FEAR AND ANXIETY

FEAR
AND
ANXIETY

Primary Triggers
of Survival
and Evolution

Paul Diel

SOCIAL SCIENCE & HISTORY DIVISION
EDUCATION & PHILOSOPHY SECTION

Hunter House Inc.
P.O. Box 847
Claremont, CA 91711

Library of Congress Cataloging in Publication Data:

Diel, Paul, 1893-1972
Fear and anxiety.
70136520
Transation of: La peur et l'angoisse.
Bibliography: p. 174
1. Anxiety. 2. Fear. I. Title.
BF575.A6D5413 1988 152.4 88-34789
ISBN 0-89793-051-7

Transated from the French by Brigitte Donvez
Editorial Director: Jennifer D. Trzyna
Copy editing: Judy Selhorst
Production Manager: Paul J. Frindt
Cover design: Qalagraphia. Image by Renee Krikken
Interior design and typesetting by 847 Communications
Text set in 10 on 12 1/2 point Century Schoolbook
Manufactured by Thomson-Shore, Inc., Dexter, MI

Manufactured in the United States of America
9 8 7 6 5 4 3 2 1   First edition

Contents

Foreword

Vital restlessness, the seed of anxiety, which is a common trait among all living beings, is the vehicle for evolutionary adaptation, because all evolutionary aims are to overcome the dissatisfaction created by the dependence of the living organism upon an environment that is often hostile. Anxiety is primarily an evolutionary phenomenon because of its immanent need to be overcome; it can become a pathological and involutionary phenomenon in the human being, who is capable of conscious choice, therefore capable of error as well. Anxiety is not only an organic phenomenon—although this study naturally should not be neglected—it is first and foremost an intrapsychic phenomenon that is intimately experienced. The study of anxiety and its transformational dynamism requires an intimate method of investigation and the author, in order to justify this method, is compelled to criticize the common tendency to view the psychic function as an epiphenomenon of the organic.[1]

The necessity for an analytical exposition in the first part of the book arose from the need to understand the fundamental hypothesis of this present work in relation to the different systems of explanation on which the research is founded: spiritualism and materialism, finalism and mechanism, classical psychology and psychoanalysis. The author attempts to extract the elements of a synthesis, biologically based not only upon somatic evolution but also upon the evolution of the psyche. The aim of this work is to demonstrate that the meaning of life can be defined without transcendental or metaphysical speculation. The value of life—its meaning and direction—lies in the effort, *the essential desire*, to overcome anxiety in all its natural and pathological forms. Life fulfills its immanent value by evolving toward a lucidity of spirit that can appraise and harmonize desires and their promise of satisfaction. Individuals are anxious, or affectively blinded, insofar as they inadequately assume the evolutionary effort that is the basis of their responsibility toward themselves. Mental illness, in every form, is the result of an affectively falsified value judgment. The tendency to make distorted and incorrect value judgments creates moralizing and amoralizing pseudocomforting ideologies on the social level that disorient individuals, and on the individual level this tendency creates a pseudocomforting self-justification, a wrong motivation that is the intimate cause of a meaningless reaction that contaminates society.

Repressing the essential desire for meaningful evolution generates individual anxiety from its beginning to its most pathological forms, and collective disorientation in its most threatening and unrecognized forms (i.e., banalization). (See Chapter 4, "Banalization," in *The Psychology of Motivation*; Diel, 1989a.) But through these very sufferings the essential desire still commands evolution. From the genetic point of view, past evolution allows faith in future evolution. Despite alarming and growing confusion, the importance of our times is reflected in the fact that the need for evolutionary and elucidating adaptation forces us to seek, by means appropriate to the study of individual and collective anxiety, the gateway to a new and genuine scientific era.

P. D.

NOTES

1. We should be pleased with the current research on the hormonal function of the brain and the physiological codetermination of the central phenomenon of anxiety. In order to guard against delusions and disappointments caused by organicist prejudice, it is important to recall these lines excerpted from the "Myth of Aesclepius," in *Symbolism in Greek Mythology* (Diel, 1980): "The ideal situation would be familiarity with the developments of both the physiological causes and the psychic motives. The confusion of modern psychiatry could well stem from its inability to work out the parallelism between these two channels of explanation, as well as from the tendency to fill the gaps in physiological explanations with psychic explanations, and the gaps in psychic explanations with physiological explanations" (note from Jane Diel, 1978).

Preface

Psychology is at present a science in the making. It has not yet succeeded in stabilizing its assets; the elaboration of its methods is not complete. This, perhaps, explains the fervor of internal conflicts and the persistence of a certain weakness, which is nonetheless characteristic of any science in gestation: the quarrel of different schools. The research is blocked, rather than shared, by the diversity of doctrines (experimental psychology, psychology of behavior, depth psychology, etc.).

How would we view physics, for instance, if it persisted in feeding such discord within itself? What if mechanistic specialists had as little information as psychologists often have of the other disciplines of their science? What if the study of optics eventually rejected the research on electricity and acoustics and paid no further attention to it? Would not the most fundamental research in psychology be concerned with the secret causes (intimate motives) of this mutual disapproval of nonobjectivity that ceaselessly feeds the quarrel between schools?

Psychology is the study of the psyche's logic, the objectivity of thought. Human thought is not exclusively logical and objective. It is susceptible to subjective errors. It is even possible—the utmost illogicality—that error be mistaken for truth. What discipline, if not the psychology of intimate motives, would know how to undertake the vital *fundamental research*: the analysis of the conditions of objectivity and nonobjectivity of the psychic quality called thought? How could one proceed without resorting to some form of self-criticism of the mind? The quarrel of the schools stems from the absence of a unifying method of objectifying self-criticism. Only by taking responsibility for this fundamental requirement can psychology successfully attain its essential aim of becoming the science of life and of its meaningful conduct.

William James, one of the most perceptive and objective psychologists of the recent past, summarized the situation in the conclusion
of his *Principles of Psychology*:

> When it is said that psychology is a natural science, care
> should be taken not to understand that it rests, without ap-
> peal, on solid foundations. Conversely, this qualification
> reveals its fragility, the fragility of a science oozing meta-
> physical critique from all its joints, the hypothesis and fun-
> damental data of which, far from having a personal and
> absolute value, are, on the contrary, answerable to theories
> overlapping them and according to which they should be re-
> thought and re-formulated. In short, making psychology a
> natural science is not exaltation but depreciation of its
> authority. We ignore even the terms by which the funda-
> mental laws—which we do not possess—should establish
> relations. Is this a science? It is a mere hope of one. We have
> but the material from which to extract that science.

The "fundamental data of psychology" that are liable to revise the
theories to which these data are answerable and that overlap psychology are epistemological by nature. Anyone wanting to rethink and
reformulate the fundamental data by means of epistemological penetration would strongly risk exposure to unanimous reprobation. Even
though psychology in its present state, as James says, "oozes metaphysics from each articulation," each attempt to revise it is discredited
as antiscientific and speculative.

*   *   *

It could be said that psychology in its present form has been elaborated
almost exclusively from the clinical observation of mental illnesses.
Psychology in its classic form is the work of great psychiatrists who
were undeniably talented but improperly equipped for fundamental
research. They naturally assumed that psychic disease is an illness
like other illnesses and has an organic cause that should be found first,
if not exclusively. Consequently, the foundation of classical psychology
is *organicism*—the prevalence of soma-matter over the psyche and the
mental function—and its method of investigation *is the observation of
the soma* at the expense of the psyche. Once psychopathological states
are declared exclusively attributable to organic causes, it then seems
obvious that the other psychic states—the functioning of the entire
psyche—are also exclusively answerable to organic causes. Neverthe-

less, *psychopathy is distinguishable from organic disease by an undeniable trait: It is a state of anxiety.* However, anxiety itself is declared to be a purely organic state, even though its undeniable intrapsychic nuance (it is intimately experienced) should invite caution in this regard. In the end, the economy of the organicist hypothesis and the requirements of clinical observation seem to authorize us to disregard this little snag and remain altogether undisturbed by it.

The truth is that the problem of anxiety—and the snag—is at the basis of the epistemological foundation of a genuine psychology and its method of observation.

Anxiety is a psychic phenomenon as much as it is an organic phenomenon. This observation is valid for any other reactive manifestation of the psychosomatic organism. Even the most abstract function —thought—possesses an underlying emotivity ranging from doubt to joy of knowledge, and, therefore, is accompanied by endocrine reactions. Among all psychic functions that are intimately experienced (desires, volitions, thoughts, etc.), anxiety is the most directly related to elementary emotivity. *Anxiety, when intimately experienced, indicates a disorder in the harmony of the whole intrapsychic function,* which is reflected in endocrine activity, thus producing somatic disorders. It is important to emphasize that somatic disorders due to anxiety follow a spasmophilia rather than a lesion. Hence, the most meticulous clinical examination of the affected organ often fails to detect any physiological dysfunction. This phenomenon is known in medicine and is classified under the name "psychosomatic symptom."

Psychiatry, by neglecting the psychic aspect of anxiety, believes it possesses an "objective" method that assures its position among other sciences, which, according to the nature of their object of study, are entitled to proceed by outer observation only.

Psychology solicits its inclusion in the sciences through the method of direct observation of behavioral disorders. This method of investigation becomes psychology's measure of scientific value. It follows that every attempt to direct attention toward the neglected intrapsyche is eventually condemned as antiscientific.

The organicist foundation and the method of outer observation are a working hypothesis that has been wrongly taken as a postulate. The anticipated economy is not achieved. Psychology, with its various branches, obviously does not succeed in establishing itself as a science. It would certainly be appropriate to revise the postulate, which is founded exclusively on the study of the organic aspect of anxiety. What if the postulate were merely a dogma? What if the snag in the approach to the problem were less negligible than is usually admitted? What if the neglected intrapsyche were as vitally significant for human beings (who live as a function of those intrapsychic data called desire, anxiety and joy) as for science, the aim of which is to understand the psyche?

*   *   *

Psychology is distinct from any other science because the object of its study is the individual, the living being. Studying subjects as if they were merely objects eliminates the essential objective—life—from scientific investigation. What do humans essentially suffer from, if not from intimately experienced anxiety?

As the existence of the intrapsyche is intimately experienced, it is too obvious to be totally neglected. Thus, psychology uses a vocabulary related to intrapsychic functions. We do not deny the existence of feelings, volitions, thoughts, and the like. However, instead of trying to specify their intimate nature and reactive range, we leave these intrapsychic data imprecise and are content to build from this imprecise base the terminology of the different processes of clinical and experimental observations.

To be fair, we should emphasize that these various directions of research each have obtained valid results. Directly observable behavior poses very complex physiological, biological, and sociological problems to scientific investigation. All these problems have a psychological aspect. Reactivity is indeed the response to extrinsic (environmental and somatic) stimuli. This response is intrapsychically elaborated from a motivating valuation. In the course of life, by observing the reactions of others, one can conclude that others have intimate motives; necessarily, then, one has previously been able to uncover them in oneself.

There is no reason to believe that the means of explanation—the psychological talent—is entirely lacking in psychologists or that it could possibly be completely eliminated in favor of an "objective" method. Thus, more or less acknowledged, it frequently plays the role of important help in the interpretation of material provided through clinical or experimental observation. The obviousness of the intrapsyche—an implicitly common foundation to all branches of psychology—led some of them to direct their attention more specifically toward the study of intimate functioning. But through faith in the *explicitly* admitted functioning (the organicist dogma, taken as a measure of scientific value), the attempts to analyze the intimate experience did not accomplish the degree of penetration set by their original intention. Instead of elaborating a special method of observation that conforms to the object of the study, these analytical schools seek the intimate experience only in others (in anxious patients), who are, therefore, the object of an investigation proceeding exclusively by outer observation (past or present traumatisms).

The organicist foundation of the life sciences and its result, the dogma of outer observation, are imputable to the following pseudosyllogism: The observation of the object is objective; the observation of the subject is subjective; any science and even psychology in order to avoid subjectivity should proceed exclusively through the observation of objects (in psychology, soma, environment, others). The conclusion would be irrefutable if the premise were not disputable.

The goal of the present study is to analyze the various manifestations of anxiety as a function of their intrapsychic causation (motivation). It was first necessary to confront the project of analysis with the major obstacle, even if that entailed attacking it ulteriorly.

It is important to emphasize that the measure of scientific value does not lie in the use of the habitually employed methods and in the exclusion of the phenomena that happen to be inaccessible to these methods. The aim of science is to search for truth about any existing phenomenon and thus about intimate psychic functioning as well. This requires the elaboration of appropriate methods, even if they are new and unusual.

PART I

Anxiety in Classical Psychology and in Introspective Psychology

1

Intrapsychic Anxiety and Its Evolutionary Dynamism

A. THE ORIGIN OF ANXIETY

The term *anxiety* is usually given too broad or too restricted a significance. It is too broad because anxiety is usually confused with fear. The distinction between them will emerge clearly from the following exposition. It is too restricted because the term includes only negative manifestations that, as a whole, form psychopathy. Pathological anxiety is only one aspect of vital *anxietude* (the term *anxietude* is used to designate the entirety of the anxiety phenomena). It is its most spectacular manifestation, but not, by far, its most important.

As paradoxical as it may seem, *anxiety is originally a vital phenomenon of formative consequence*. Its pathological functioning, although spectacular, can be understood only through its original function, which is more difficult to discern because of its long-term evolutionary nature.

To live is to feel. To feel is to oscillate between a state of dissatisfaction and a state of satisfaction. These opposite states are manifested in humans as two clearly differentiated feelings: anxiety and joy. As human life is a later manifestation of evolution, the range of feelings and their oscillation between joy and anxiety can be genetically understood only from the elementary emotivity governing animal life. Even at the human level the differentiated feelings remain in part emotive and unconscious, with an aspiration to conscious lucidity and to the faculty of voluntary and foreseeing control.

From the perspective of evolution, life does not seem to have any meaning other than to overcome *fundamental restlessness,* the seed of anxiety. Restlessness is the characteristic trait common to all living beings; it is caused by their dependence upon a surrounding world that is liable to hinder the satisfaction of their vital needs. The body is the intermediary between restlessness experienced in the moment and the world indirectly perceived. Restlessness is expressed through the soma, but not without first imprinting itself, and this impression constitutes psychic life. The somatic and the psychic have been inseparable since the very beginning and remain so throughout evolution, which can be looked upon as the effort to adapt the living being to a hostile environment.

Biology studies the evolutionary adaptation of the body. Morphological variations, however, are simply observable indicators of an essential transformation that relates to the psychic life not directly observable. Insofar as the effort to adapt tends to overcome fundamental restlessness, more sensitized forms of psychic life are always created; their growing complexity is a source of new anxiety-laden difficulties. Fundamental restlessness differentiates into multiple dissatisfactions, to which correspond multiple and intensified anxieties requiring more lucid and voluntary psychic functions for their dissolution.

Anxiety-laden restlessness is the *driving force of evolution* in its psychic form. It constitutes the *transformational dynamism of anxiety.* The biogenetic dynamism of anxiety, in the pursuit of a means of assuagement, evolutionally creates the instinctive foresight of the animal; as it proceeds with its evolutionary growth, it eventually generates the functioning of the higher psyche: the half-conscious, half-unconscious structuralization of the human psyche. This structuralization forms a unit, a "whole," because its unitary origin is fundamental restlessness. It is higher because it is more lucid and thereby more efficient in the pursuit of assuagement. The vehicle for evolution, anxiety—or psychic suffering (to be distinguished from pathological anxietude appearing only in humans)—is a *natural phenomenon.*

Human anxiety, in its natural form, is on one hand *a torment of dissatisfaction* pursuing assuagement in the most intense satisfaction: joy (sublimation, sound formation of the character). On the other hand, it is *a state of disorientation,* an affective blindness, to be evolutionarily overcome through an elucidating orientation (spiritualization, formation of right ideas). However, on the half-conscious level, another split occurs in connection with the transformational dynamism of anxiety; the means of assuagement are no longer triggered automatically but by way of thought, and are therefore subject to error. The dynamism of anxiety is no longer exclusively evolutionary; it can become involutionary. Because the evolutionary effort leads to the assuagement of anxiety, any lessening or deficiency of that effort—which is half voluntary—leads to the opposite of assuagement: the exaltation of anxiety. *Perversion* occurs instead of sublimation-spiritualization. Perverse exaltation relates to anxiety not only as a form of torment, but also as an aspect of vital disorientation. Exalted anxiety is meaningless, unhealthy, pathological. The involutionary and pathological exaltation of anxiety, possible only at the human level of evolution, becomes the principle of psychic distortion and its morbid consequences at both individual and social levels.

Understanding the functioning of the human psyche, the true task of psychology, is, therefore, the ability to develop from fundamental restlessness—the seed of anxiety—the evolutionary genesis of higher functions and their risk of perversion. All multiple forms of surmounted or exalted anxiety, which have a common root in vital restlessness and its transformational dynamism, the multiple joys and anxieties of humankind, do not exist independently of each other. They are the result of unremitting intrapsychic work, sometimes sublimative, sometimes perverting. Sublimations and perversions become motives for future actions. Created by half-lucid thought, motives are not static. *The sublime is susceptible to perversion, the perverse can be sublimated.* Upon these incessant transformations rests the destiny of humankind.

Anxiety in its intimately experienced, intrapsychic form is the most important problem of life. Is it not correct to say that to understand anxiety from its biopsychic roots all the way to the diversity of forms it is likely to take in the partially conscious psyche of the human being is also to understand the nature of the evolutionary impulse right down to its means of realization, thereby glimpsing the meaning of life and its immanent value?

B. INTRAPSYCHIC ANXIETY: A SYSTEMATIC STUDY

This last statement is a hypothetical synthesis. This hypothesis might be economical enough to be worth considering, but is it verifiable? To verify it, it is important to inquire whether its economical value can be established, in detail, from animal to human life. The intent of the following study is to provide this demonstration.

However, to grasp and classify the details of the problem of intrapsychic anxiety in its intimately experienced form, the demonstration
requires a method of investigation that can penetrate the intrapsyche.
Life imposes its problems and forces science to develop its method.
Should the initial hypothesis prove correct, anxiety in its directly experienced form would be the central problem imposed upon science by
life, for life's only goal through evolution is to overcome anxiety.

In order to understand the true nature of intrapsychic anxiety as
a motivating force, all intimate motivations, the totality of phenomena
constituting intimate life, should be studied. In this respect, it is important to state that the hypothetical synthesis issued here is the
result of a previous study of motivations (see Diel, 1989a).

Intimate life undoubtedly exists. Refusing to study it with an appropriate method has very serious consequences. Allegedly incapable
of approaching the intrapsyche systematically, psychological observation, which is restricted only to the study of organic anxiety, risks never
finding a wide enough base to further the reasoning—as any science
should—from the analysis of observable facts to the synthesis and,
eventually, to the discovery of laws. Consequently, the innovative tendency toward intrapsychic analysis is spreading gradually in the hope
of establishing a general and genetic theory of psychic functioning. All
current forms of psychoanalysis use an interpretative method to this
end, which in fact contains a kind of introspection, neither acknowledged nor systematically used, of which classical psychology, supported by its ideal of objectivity, never fails to disapprove.

To distinguish the analysis of motivations, which provides the
basis for the initial synthesis hypothetically proposed, from all other
forms of psychic investigation, it is useful to introduce, for the study of
motives, the designation *intimate observation*.

*Classical psychology proposes outer observation as a principle of
objectivity*. It sees the principle of nonobjectivity in self-observation,
supposedly exclusively morbid. Intimate observation, as a *method* of
investigation, will look for the principle of objectivity that exists *in the
conscience of the subject* as the psychic quality called *impartiality*. Systematically guided, intimate observation will have to demonstrate that
the principle of nonobjectivity, *partiality*, is not only peculiar to morbid
introspection. The psychic phenomenon of partiality can, for that matter, render the observation of the outer world nonobjective and, especially, the observation of others—the more or less partial observation
of the behavior of others.

Partiality is the result of a disoriented affectivity, blinded by intimate "anxietude." The principle of objectivity can reside only in the objectivization of the subject acquired by cleansing the affect. Regardless of the difference in perspective, the common link is the concern for objectivity, which leaves the hope that finding a common ground may not be totally impossible. It is important to set aside the theory of anxiety momentarily in order to clarify first the position we are taking in regard to classical psychology.

*   *   *

Morbid introspection should not be confused with intimate observation, as it is unquestionably the opposite of any objectivity. However, the existence of morbid introspection proves nothing against the possibility of objective introspection; on the contrary, it shows the pitfall to avoid. Moreover, this pitfall should be studied, for it is the true cause of nonobjectivity toward oneself and, consequently, toward one's own psyche and its functioning. Morbid introspection is the effect of pathological anxiety; to maintain that the psychologist should avoid self-introspection because of the risk of nonobjectivity also affirms that some degree of insurmountable pathological anxiety exists in every human being. To establish that distorting anxiety exists in everyone's conscience, even that of the psychologist, is the supreme wisdom of psychology. This observation defines the true problem of psychology: the existence of intrapsychic anxiety. By claiming intrapsychic anxiety — principle of nonobjectivity toward oneself—insurmountable, do we not, in effect, transform the intrapsyche's anxiety into an anxiety of confronting the intrapsyche, thus declaring the true problem of psychology insolvable and inaccessible?

This is why Auguste Comte, the first to start the anathema, who saw very clearly that psychology without introspection would hardly be possible, and who believed that it would be necessarily subjective if not morbid, turned the problem around by purely and simply excluding psychology from the domain of science. Classical psychology, wishing to withdraw the self-condemnation, accepts the anathema entirely but applies it exclusively to intimate observation.

Is this the historical cause of the disconcerting show offered by a science divided by irreconcilable doctrines that can agree on only a single point: the condemnation of intimate observation? This unanimous reprobation is hardly advantageous to psychology. This common reprobation is not the basic error that condemns, in an unjustifiable way, the most efficient and specific tool of psychological research?

Whether justified or unjustifiable, the condemnation of introspection acts against psychology; if justified, it deprives the research of its object (which is intimate in nature), thus putting into question the possibility of a genuine knowledge of the psyche and the scientific scope of psychology. If unjustifiable, the reprobation would be the result of a subjective prejudice disguised as an objective judgment. What is the origin of the specific characteristic of this particularly obsessing prejudice that inserts itself at the core of the study of the psyche, precisely where it should not be seen? This reaction of rejection could result only from some intimate anxiety, the nature of which will be gradually specified in the course of the present study of the various forms of intrapsychic anxiety.

We can establish that intimate observation is truly humankind's most natural and essential function; this is why it generally operates instinctively and unconsciously. Introspection is no less indispensable to the psyche than food and digestion are to the body. The psyche (the entirety of psychic functions—desires, volitions, thoughts, and so forth) is "fed" by the influx of excitations; their "digestion," is accomplished as *an intrapsychic work* requiring a certain degree of introspective attention, which does not usually reach the threshold of consciousness for the completion of the process. In its sane form, any function of the mind, while processing "intrapsychic digestion," tends toward clarity. Its instinctive work can, however, be disturbed by the intrusion of insufficiently lucid thought that results in *morbid introspection, the genuine cause of all pathological distortions* of the psyche.

To understand the causes of the distortion of the psyche is the same as the process of *elucidating introspection*. The aim of the preliminary elaboration of introspection (conscious or instinctive) concerns not only the motives of future actions (and, therefore, all aspects of interhuman and social activity), but also the relations of mutual understanding or misunderstanding. The motives that animate others and determine their character (the result of their own intimate elaboration) can be understood only through *projective introspection* (through the projection of instinctive or lucid knowledge, acquired through a preliminary self-observation). *Morbid introspection determines the morbid interpretation of oneself and others*; a lucid self-observation allows a lucid understanding of the intentions and character of others. The interpretation of the character of others can become objective and scientific when self-observation has become systematic.

The scope of the problem goes beyond one's own relation to oneself; it extends to human interreactions. This justifies the opinion

of a great scientist, who, although not a psychologist by profession, is
gifted with an acuteness of penetration that is exemplary in all forms
of research. Albert Einstein says in a letter to the author dated June
2nd, 1946 (translated from the German): "Pavlov and Behaviorism are
using the sole psychological method that could be called 'objective,' but
it only permits the study of the surface of psychic phenomena. In all
other methods of psychological investigation, introspection, the effort
to render conscious intimately experienced psychic manifestations,
plays an essential role, if only in an indirect way; and I really hold the
attempted camouflage of this principal source of psychological knowledge to be a fashionable disease."

*   *   *

It would be preferable to study intrapsychic anxiety without the need
to introduce the distressing question concerning which method to use.
The problem of introspection is inherent to psychology from its most
obscure origin, and its insufficient elucidation still weighs upon the
development of human sciences. The ancient mythical and philosophical prescription "Know thyself" is replaced by the anathema that
proclaims self-knowledge to be the most antiscientific of all human
ventures. Rather than making an attempt to surpass the prescientific
stage by a systematic elaboration of self-knowledge, the measure of
scientific value has been sought in a radical opposition to the profound
intuition from which springs the origin of humankind's reflection upon
itself and its destiny. The result is failure to penetrate to an understanding of the essential aspect of human problems. It is interesting to
note, however, that intimate observation never ceases to find defenders
among the most reputable psychologists. Numerous are the testimo-
nies that stand out as milestones in the history of psychology to the
present time.

It would suffice to quote a few lines written by the distinguished
psychiatrist H. Baruk (1950):

> In these objective methods, the observer studies phe-
> nomena from *outside*, without, in fact, participating in the
> intimate life which animates them. These methods of study
> are excellent for all physical manifestations and also for cer-
> tain elementary psychological factors including measurable
> elements which are likely to be analyzed impartially from
> the outside. But how does one understand, with this meth-
> od, the deepest feelings prompting individuals and entire
> societies *to act?* How can we perceive the reactions of good

and evil? Imagine, for example, an observer who wants to study the consequences of fairness and unfairness. If he has not experienced the suffering of unfairness *in himself* he won't have the strength to open his eyes and to investigate, in detail, conflicts that will seem uninteresting to him. If there isn't within him a powerful affective drive to possibly alleviate the suffering of unfairness he won't be able to undertake any experiment.

...One can have certain impressions about somebody—inclinations—without knowing why. The psychological factors which trigger these impressions remain obscure, subconscious but active, nonetheless. Little by little they may become clearer; these impressions might come from different circumstances or attitudes that may have left a good or bad memory. Now it is no longer a vague impression. We know the why. The question is being refined. That is the transition from *the subconscious to the conscious.* This work presupposes a certain mental work of refinement and reflection; it also requires *a perfect sincerity toward oneself.* One must not be afraid to acknowledge impressions that one ordinarily denies, in order to discover without fear one's own weaknesses and to know them better by discovering their causes. It is the essential condition of the harmony of personality, self-mastery and, therefore, freedom.

Isn't this an apologia of intimate observation? (At this point, it is not important to know whether or not this quote contains an exact description of the process, as it would be impossible to describe the method in so few lines.)

What is important to extract from this quote is the perfect formulation that indicates the essential condition of all observation of psychic intimacy: in order to discover without fear one's own weaknesses and to know them better by discovering their causes. The difficulty of intimate observation, like the cause of the aversion to its systematic use, lies in the fact that in the intrapsyche, in all human beings without exception, there is a tendency to deny one's own weaknesses because their discovery, without the spiritualizing force (only possibility for objectivity), is likely to trigger a painful, unbearable feeling, an anxiety that is likely to develop into terror. This terror of recognizing one's own multiple weaknesses has an exclusively intrapsychic source; it is anxiety in its most essential and intimate form. No outside

observation will ever succeed in uncovering it. Behavior only expresses the multiple weaknesses that are conditioned by surrounding difficulties. But these multiple weaknesses, which are outwardly
observable, also have an intrapsychic cause that lies in the fact that
the defense energy is inhibited or absorbed by multiple accidental
anxieties (worry, impatience, intimidation, resentment, etc.). To not
recognize the intimate motives of behavioral weaknesses makes one
incapable of overcoming the intrapsychic failing, the inhibition of energy. *The anxiety of recognition is, therefore, the essential form in which
all negative energy of multiple and accidental anxieties is concentrated.*
Overcoming this essential denial of truth toward oneself and the tendency of nonrecognition of the intimate cause of often-faulty human behavior is thus depriving multiple anxieties (secret motives of the
failings) of the perverse support that protects them from spiritualizing
recognition and from objectivizing observation. It makes multiple
anxieties analyzable. The theory of the method of intimate observation
does not lie outside a systematic study of intrapsychic anxiety; on the
contrary, it enters into the objective study of the anxiety-laden intrapsyche.

*   *   *

With nonrecognition treated as a method, the anathema that weighed
upon the study of intrapsychic anxiety found its most concentrated expression in the theories of James Lange and Brissaud. In these two
theories, the existence of the intrapsyche is denied or, at least, considered an insignificant fact.

    Brissaud makes a distinction between anxiousness and anxiety.
He neglects the usual and linguistic meanings of the two terms and
gives them a restricted significance with the sole purpose of establishing a theory in which anxiety, in its intimately experienced form,
is excluded. Anxiety, according to Brissaud, is the totality of organic
disturbances; anxiousness is the affective repercussion of organic anxiety. This repercussion certainly exists. It belongs in the phenomenon
known as "cenesthesia," the reverberations that organic sensations
have upon affective life.

    However, anxiety-laden cenesthesia, or hypochondria, is merely
one of the multiple forms of intimate anxiety. By neglecting all other
manifestations of psychic anxiety and by making cenesthetic anxiety—
called anxiousness or "inner anxiety"—the only inner phenomenon to
be studied, the theory succeeds wonderfully in shifting the emphasis
from the inner to the outer. Since cenesthetic anxiousness is only the

inner reverberation of organic and peripheral disturbance, would it not be consistent to conclude, from the premises thus established for the purpose, that to thoroughly study the problem it suffices to consider only the outer problem, which is called, in spite of everything, "anxiety"? The idea becomes even more substantiated as physiology localizes the organic cause of affective and cognitive phenomena in various nervous centers. According to Brissaud, the cenesthetic anxiety called "anxiousness" is a cerebral phenomenon and the organic problem of "anxiety" is a bulbar phenomenon. Therefore, all forms of anxiety, whether inner or peripheral, are reduced to organic causes. Discussion of the general theory of localizations or this particular hypothesis of localization is not our intention here, but it should be said that the physiological aspect of the problem should be neither neglected nor mistaken for its psychological facet.

Juliette Boutonnier (1945), in her interesting work on anxiety, protests against this confusion. She clearly expresses the imperative objection to Brissaud's theory, which is still in vogue, albeit in a rather attenuated form. She says: "To make or to appear to make anxiety into a physical sensation, a somatic state and nothing more, is a mistake; in any event, it influences the mind to make one." She adds: "The definition thus presented is incomplete and proceeds from an obsolete method which actually leads to a dead end; because, for not having explained anxiety and for labeling it 'organic'—which should have rid psychology of it—it reappears in anxiousness for which one is always tempted, and for a good reason, to utter the word anxiety" (p. 29).

The theory of Lange eliminates the psychic problem of anxiety even more thoroughly. According to this theory, the affectivity (elementary emotions and nuanced feelings, even cenesthesia), or the whole psychic functioning, is merely an organic and peripheral epiphenomenon. The theory can be summarized by the same paradox that assured its success, even outside the strictly scientific milieu: "We don't cry because we are sad, we are sad because we cry." It is the most radical attempt to justify the tendency to degrade the intrapsyche in favor of the organic. It is also the most perfect and most typical example of a speculative and arbitrary misinterpretation invented solely for the purpose and elevated to a theory outside the realm of any experimentation. This paradox, disguised as a theory, triggered a profuse discussion that resulted in its rejection, especially after the critiques of Cannon and Sherington. However, it cannot be said that the final failure of this excessive doctrine succeeded in discrediting the dogma of organic prevalence.

Direct experience, however, teaches anyone that in a state of outwardly conditioned dejection caused, for instance, by the loss of a loved
one, tears will spurt following the aggravation of the retrospective form
of anxiety called grief. The least amount of intimate observation will
demonstrate that grief is aggravated to tears only in moments when to
this intimate cause of a general order is added an entire chain of intimate causes of a more particular order, which is the imaginative
evocation of memories by which one remains affectively tied to a
deceased. In bringing the analysis of this intimate causation further,
we can notice that the detailed cause of tears (the motives) may be of
a very different and often contradictory nature: genuine affliction,
remorse, anxiety about future loneliness, self-pity, and so on. Motives
of a less respectable nature could be added, such as the need to
dramatize one's personal suffering. Some motives that provoke the
tears could assume an illogical or magical character, such as conceiv-
ing that the deceased remains a witness even beyond the grave and it
is important to appease him by the magnitude of the suffering. In view
of the infinite wealth of this more or less secret causation, what an ab-
surdity to see only the insignificant effect of lachrymal secretion! But
it is very tempting, in the face of this motivation partly masked because too painful to be easily disclosed and confessed, to keep to the
outwardly observable physiological effect in order to avoid confronting
the intimacy of the human psyche. Is it not significant that such a long
and complicated discussion was required to eliminate a mistake that
is glaringly obvious with the least effort of intimate observation?

The genuine measure of the value of a science is not its means of
study, the applied observation—outer or intimate—but its theoretical
and practical fruitfulness. If the technical application that resulted
from physical theories were successful only in building apparatuses
unable to function, these theories would be disproved by their sterility
and falsity. However, the theories of classical psychology do not meet
at all with practical reality—that is to say, the cure of psychic illnesses—because they do not stem from psychic reality. Classical psychology indeed produced a psycho-technique. But is it not justified to
expect much more than a professional orientation from psychology?
Psychology, by exploring the intrapsyche, which is the genuine realm
of its research, meets the most vitally important phenomenon, the anxiety-laden disorientation. How could psychology retreat from the need
to view this phenomenon as a problem to be solved? By confronting this
intimate problem, psychological theory will meet the living reality, because to resolve it is to elucidate the conditions of a nonanxious orien-

tation: the orientation toward the meaning of life.

What would we say of a physical science that is content to deal with only theoretically minor and practically most urgent problems, but would retreat from the task of expanding the investigation to the boundaries of the universe in its cosmic and atomic aspects? Instead of condescending to imitate physics and its methods slavishly, psychology should rather aim to equal the magnificent scope of its discoveries. It should attempt to elaborate an appropriate method with the ability to penetrate the nature of psychic intimacy from the limits of the *vital universe* all the way to the origin of life, in order to uncover the laws of intrapsychic causation or the laws of motivation from these biological data. Thus, psychology would be led from the limits of the vital universe to the limits of the *inner universe* to the usually unfathomable depths of the extraconscious, where the motives seem to become lost in an imponderable infinity and where their advance becomes as indeterminable by ordinary means as the advance of corpuscles in physics.

The theoretical expansion of observed facts and their generalization into a law is proper to all scientific method and is even a crowning achievement. Physics excels in the process of systematic expansion that leads it to theories that are no longer verifiable through direct observation but only by the power of their coherent explanation. Psychology will not successfully expand into a comprehensive body of theory unless it accepts the observation of the intrapsyche, where the differentiation of the emotive into motives is elaborated; this differentiation is evolutionary dynamism.

All human feelings amount to anxiety and its demand for assuagement. If feelings cannot be observed and their subjectively experienced intrapsychic nuance cannot be established, there is no hope that psychology will arrive at a coherent theory, *for the intrapsychic nuance is the only characteristic feature that can link the elementary emotions that prompt the animal to the feelings that stir human beings before actively putting them into motion.* Since the intimate nuance of animal emotions is not directly observable, it can be incorporated, in accordance with the study of the indeterminable phenomena in atomic physics, into a coherent theory only from the observation of the intimate nuance of human feelings and their differential features, the common source of which is the anxiety to overcome.

The initial hypothesis has been established with this understanding. We then need to know if intimate observation of the intrapsyche and anxiety and the means to overcome it can exceed the subjectivity of which the so-called objective methods disapprove.

* * *

Psychology as a whole and any domain of its theoretical or practical research remains tributary to intimate observation. A comparison with
the systematic process used in physics is again imperative. What allows physics to expand its questioning to the limits of the knowable
and what provides it with the possibility of finding the solution to its
problems (the growing boldness of which ceaselessly emerges from its
theoretical comprehensive vision) is *the precise definition of its terminology* rather than the possibility of using quantitative measure-
ment that can be mathematically formulated. Language offers to
science terms such as *force, energy, work, mass, speed*, and *acceleration*,
terms that were created from a prescientific observation of the outer
world. These terms are not accepted as such by physics, but undergo
an effort of precision that assures them a special and clearly defined
significance.

    Language offers a whole terminology to psychology, also. Instead
of defining the terms that are biogenetic in nature, psychology uses the
terms—*drive, instinct, emotion, affectivity, fear, anxiety*, and so on—
without particular distinction. After the fashion of philosophy, from
which it has developed, psychology features certain functions—
thought, will, feeling—and treats them as entities that, because they
are genetically unexplained, appear to be of occult origin. (In preconscious functions, discriminating features are not well established, so
the functions remain confused because of their common genetic origin;
conversely, in the functions of the conscious psyche, the discriminating
features are exaggerated and the common genesis is neglected.)

    The employment of a poorly defined vocabulary entails a constant
effort of revision without the attainment of a final solution. Each
author is forced to refer to his or her predecessors, either by agreeing
with their opinions or by contesting them, which results in a complicated body of interminable quotes and discussions without end. Physics is in constant progress precisely because its terminology, firmly
established and mathematically formulated, permits the unquestionable elimination of any deviations, which allows each researcher to
continue the common work from where the predecessor left off. Short
of the privilege to express itself in mathematical formulas, psychology
should all the more exercise its own privilege of expressing itself in
genetic formulations, in order to define its concepts once and for all.
Discussion may never be eliminated completely from psychological research; certainly its exclusion is not possible in the present state of psychology. Therefore, it is more desirable that discussion emerge from a

live and direct common method of investigation of psychic phenomena rather than from the contradiction of emitted opinions. The recourse to discussion, always unfortunate, should be regarded as a last resort, instead of being promoted to the level of a methodological ideal, as is too often the case.

Endless discussion succeeds only in troubling the limpidity of prescientific wisdom, which is the ancestral creator of psychological terminology. In that respect, it is more instructive to lend an attentive ear to certain linguistic developments that point to an underlying genetic vision. It is pertinent to recall the example in which the entire genesis of the psyche is summarized: The motion of inanimate bodies is lawfully regulated by forces that determine the reaction to shock (shift of form or location). The animate soma, the psychosomatic organism is—as a body—exposed to the same shock; but as animate, it is *sensitized* to the shock. The shock stimulates the psyche and the reaction acquires an entirely different characteristic. The stimulation excites the psyche to externalize and it is felt as *excitation*. If the somatic reaction does not succeed in responding appropriately there is an intrapsychic motion. The inappropriate externalization of the motion is intimately perceived and the psyche is roused ("moved"). This internalized motion creates an energetic *tension* in the psyche, an anticipation, the sensation of *time* flowing within dissatisfaction that occurs until the moment when an appropriate reaction is achieved: reaction to excitation. Dissatisfaction creates the notion of time. Anticipation, imbued with vital restlessness, is also poised for satisfaction, through *attention* to the outer world. Insofar as this attention does not successfully find the opportunity of a satisfying release for the internalized motion—for the emotion—the attention itself remains internalized. It becomes *intention* in charge of elucidating and preparing a future release in spite of present obstacles. Now, this intention that prepares future action is the *emotive*, which is gradually differentiated in the multiplicity of more or less clear *motives*. These linguistic observations proceed as much from the psychogenetic phenomenon as from a preconscious introspection, not morbid but, on the contrary, extremely lucid.[1]

The obvious objection is that these are purely formal analogies. But such an objection only veils the gravity of the problem in order to avoid confronting it. It is inconceivable that the linguistic genius (examples of which can be found in all languages) could have "played" with words before creating them. The point here is the creative power of language. Conversely, to deny the extent of the problem is an easy and futile game, for it decides on its own the method to follow. The problem imposed upon psychology by the existence of its own preconsciously elaborated terminology forces the whole problem of the extraconscious functioning of the psyche to unfold. How can the functioning of the psyche be theoretically reconstructed to explain explicitly the implicit ability to *re-create the story of vital evolution through linguistic allusions?*

Yet we should take into consideration the fact that these preconsciously inspired allusions, which are more than conscious (superconscious), remain very incomplete in many other ways. Psychology should exert itself to follow the track of linguistic prescience and even to fill its gaps. This primary condition must be met for the inner world science to match the outer world science successfully in precision and cohesion. If we could theoretically and completely reconstruct the evolutionary development of higher functions from elementary functions, a coherent and comprehensive vision would result, supported by a kind of functional calculus that would include the genetic hierarchy of psychic functioning. This calculus, though deprived of quantitative exactitude, is very rich in qualitative precision (see "Psychological Calculus," in *The Psychology of Motivation*; Diel, 1989a). In psychology, as in physics, the various manifestations of underlying force can be explained as a function of one or many of the other manifestations, because of their mutual implication. As opposed to physics, the underlying force common to all vital and psychic phenomena is immediately experienced in the form of an energetic tension, a restlessness seeking its assuagement, which *is anxiety in its most elementary form: a transformational dynamism, the principle of evolution.*

In order to elaborate a complete theory of psychic functioning and to establish (parallel to the functional formulas of physics) interfunctional formulations, obviously psychology should knowingly resort to the method that allowed language to elaborate a psychological terminology in which the genetic dependency of functions is already at least partly sketched out and implied. If language could preestablish a terminology (speed, acceleration, and so forth) usable in physics (provided the terms are transformed into precise definitions, clearly delineated and functionally linked), it is evident that the linguistic process probably drew its inspiration from a preconscious method of outside observation. But is it not also clear that the psychological terminology—established since very remote times by the most varied languages and yet proven efficient enough to serve as a basis for psychologists' research—could be primitively elaborated only from an intimate observation of the intrapsyche? The simple fact that language lends to psychologists differential terms such as *fear* and *anxiety* testifies to the primitive existence of intimate observation; no outer observation could have disclosed the nature of this intimate difference, which will be defined explicitly later.

Contrary to what occurs in physics, the raw vocabulary of psychological language (which still contains much misunderstood nuance) is improperly considered as a sufficient research base. Psychology neglects to use intimate observation, the only appropriate method to raise the implicit definitions of the primitive terminology to knowingly explicit definitions. As a result, objective psychological theories, particularly theories about anxiety, which suffer from indistinct definitions of the various functions of emotional life, remain tainted with inexactitudes and confusions.

The first part of the present work proposes a critical revision of the various theories of anxiety that are based exclusively on clinical observation and use a terminology that has been established without prior definition. This will give the opportunity for a confrontation that gradually specifies the outlined proposition and closely examines the various problems involved, the prevalence of intrapsychic anxiety, the orientation in respect to the diversity of its forms, the exposition of the method of intimate investigation, and its emphasis owing to the definitions it requires and permits to establish.

The elements thus clearly presented in a critical analysis will be used in a unified synthesis that will follow the steps of the genesis of psychic functioning, starting with the fundamental restlessness to the unfolding of foreseeing and lucid functions. It will attempt to demonstrate that evolutionary adaptation, although triggered by the threat of surrounding obstacles and dangers, is *fundamentally due to the transformational dynamism of anxiety.*

NOTES

1. The linguistic links in this passage are much more apparent in French.

2

Anxiety in Classical Psychology

Classical psychology categorizes anxiety as an emotion. By so doing, neither anxiety nor emotion is clearly defined. Anxiety is constantly confused with fear, and elementary emotion with human affectivity.

To analyze all the theories expressed by the classical school would be impossible and superfluous because they have the common tendency, as previously mentioned, to transpose the study from the psychological to the physiological plane, believing that this mere transposition guarantees the objectivity of the research. In his *Essai sur les emotions*, Lange (1895) writes, "Emotions should be objectively studied and one ought to research what physiological phenomena accompany them." The guiding principle common to all classical psychological research is thus concisely expressed.

To illustrate this analysis, the classical theory of anxiety as presented by both Ribot and Dumas will suffice. This limited choice is justified by the diametrically opposed positions of these two authors. Ribot, although influenced by Lange's theory, is not entirely subject to its influence. For Ribot, the "objective" study of emotions is a means, if not an outright pretext, to allow him to formulate theoretical views with the aim of reconstituting the genesis of all psychic functions. In Dumas's theory, on the other hand, the influence of the theory of physiology is paramount. He led Lange's theory to triumph in France, only to reject it later; still, he remains deeply influenced by its concepts. Dumas is attempting to eliminate any endeavor to expand the theory of emotions, which he considers incompatible with objective research. Dumas, more than anyone else, sought the ideal of objectivity by taking the route of completely excluding psychic phenomena in favor of organic manifestations.

A. RIBOT'S THEORY OF ANXIETY

Ribot (1925, p. 139), in his *Psychologie des sentiments*, places anxiety—usually confused with fear in classical psychology—in the category of emotions; of these he studied especially fear, anger, tender emotion, egoist emotion, and sexual emotion. This points to the existence of a rather arbitrary and incoherent juxtaposition of various psychic functions very different in nature and origin. According to Ribot, these five psychic states possess the character of primary and irreducible emotions, a character he sometimes gives to other states, such as the instinct for mimicry, the instinct for play, and a propensity for knowledge (p. 205). It should be obvious that, under these conditions, any psychic phenomenon could be categorized as primary and irreducible.

According to Ribot, there is a *primitive fear*, instinctive and unconscious, that is senior to any individual experience, and a *secondary fear*, conscious and reasoned, that is postexperiential (p. 217). The second, *more or less conscious and reasoned, fear is human anxiety*. There is no question that the distinction between a more or less conscious fear and a primitive and instinctive fear requires that only the latter be recognized as elementary emotivity already observable in the preconscious level of the animal. For Ribot, nonetheless, the primitive fear is the fear "of the unknown, of the darkness, of mysterious powers." The truth is, the animal does not know this form of fear, which, far from being a primitive emotion, is, on the contrary, *a state of anxiety, a fear created by the imagination*. It seems legitimate to affirm, henceforth, that in Ribot's classification, animal fear is confused with human anxiety.

*   *   *

The genetic intention of Ribot's theory is clearly recognizable in his attempt to derive from elementary emotions all the higher psychic functions: social, moral, religious, aesthetic, and intellectual. Ribot characterizes these higher and derived feelings as "complex emotions" (p. 281). He distinguishes the composition of a complex emotion according to mix and combination. Thus, for Ribot, hate is quite justifiably a degenerate form of animal aggression produced by a cessation of spiritualizing evolution.

No less perspicacious is Ribot's idea that the conflicts of the human psyche are the result of antagonism between emotions (stopped in evolutionary development) and cogitation (intellectualized emotion) (p. 291). The intrapsychic conflict that begins at the human level is thus recognized as imputable to *the ambivalence of emotional energy that is partially affectively blinded and partially spiritualized.* Consequently, we must admit that this conflicting situation is a danger at the human level, which henceforth resides within the intimacy of the psyche and, insofar as the intimate conflict is not overcome, becomes a source of intrapsychic anxiety in its multiple forms. Is there another way to overcome this anxiety-laden conflict other than by using lucid and spiritualized energy to fight the causes of the "cessation in the development of emotional energy"? (It might be argued that any person in a state of conflict tries to do this more or less lucidly without having to be a professional psychologist.) If Ribot, after having very perspicaciously established the premise, does not draw this conclusion, which would have led him to establish the necessity of intimate observation and intrapsychic control, it is because he was himself the victim of a "cessation," an interdict, imposed by the dogma of the classical school and consisting of the confusion of the intrapsyche with an organic "inner." After having spoken about the inner and outer conditions of emotions, Ribot says on the subject: "It is easy to see that these intrapsychic conditions are reduced to what is designated by inner, organic, vital sensations" (p. 120). It is the reduction of the intrapsyche to cenesthetic sensations, already mentioned in Brissaud's material. Ribot defines cenesthesia as: "Consciousness of our body, result of chemical actions which occur in the tissues and liquids of the organism"(p. 437).

Therefore, it is not surprising that Ribot, having glimpsed that the cause of psychic degeneration is the cessation of the evolutionary development of emotivity toward a spiritual lucidity capable of control and valuation, concludes as follows: "This degeneration is essentially an organic downfall, a state of physiological misery that is first and foremost translated by some alterations in the order of emotions, tendencies, actions and movements. But the intelligence sustains the shock much better and sometimes remains unharmed"(p. 437).

Thus prevented from using the method of spiritualizing objectivation, which is considered too subjective, Ribot proposes the following method: "Track each of these feelings back to their origin; strive to determine their nature and follow their development throughout the greater stages with the help of the documentation provided by ethnology, history of customs, religions, aesthetic and scientific culture; avoid the vague and the *a priori* without becoming lost in the inextricable mass of facts"(p. 280).

It is no longer the method of observation of the organic, which obviously does not go very far, but it is a method that is said to be objective because it proceeds from the outside. This can go very far and for that reason can lead only to the most subjective deviation. It leaves the field open for a wide range of interpretation. It is important to state in honor of Ribot, who is characterized by a very sober and perspicacious discourse, that no such method is used in his works, so one is tempted to believe that he proposed it only to mask his true process of investigation and expansion for fear he would be criticized for being too speculative; it is certainly not with the help of an interpretation of historical documents that Ribot found, for instance, the idea of a genetic transformation of simple emotions into complex emotions, or that he could recognize the insufficient spiritualization of emotional energy as a cause of the intrapsychic conflict. The true process used by Ribot (as, moreover, by all psychologists of talent) is based, short of a genuine method of intimate observation, on a certain gift of introspection.

This psychological talent always existed. It leads one to ask the question: *How can I explain the meaning of such and such intimate motive in the most plausible manner?* However, *plausible* doesn't necessarily mean *true*. This method of orientation in relation to the intrapsyche (in as much as we can call it a "method") brings to mind the method of trial and error, a groping for orientation in space that is proper to all primitive beings deprived of vision. As long as human beings remain deprived of a methodically sharpened "inner vision," this psychological talent will produce only a more or less amusing interpretative and literary game that is, moreover, insufficient for the elaboration of a science.

*   *   *

Human anxiety is a derived form of fear. It is fear represented and prolonged in the imagination. Consequently, a genetic relation should exist between human anxiety and animal emotivity. First, a definition of elementary fear is necessary to establish its various forms, even before we approach the analysis of human anxiety with the help of intimate observation.

According to the usual meaning, the term *emotion* indicates an abrupt rupture in the psychophysical balance manifesting under the influence of an actual danger. *At the level of the animal's elementary emotion, the emotional shock will always be due to a present, vital danger, to a mortal peril.* (In classical psychology, it is usual to distinguish emotion from emotional shock.) But this distinction does not apply to the elementary emotion of the animal, especially the primitive animal. It is justified only in regard to human emotivity, characterized by a prolonged reverberation of the shock. This prolonged reverberation is human anxiety, which is no longer an elementary emotion but an emotional agitation of imaginative origin and very often of pathological consequences.

Human emotional agitation belongs to the sphere of complex feelings and blinded affectivity. Emotional agitation is therefore unfit to serve as a base for an analysis of elementary emotion.

*   *   *

To obtain a valid classification of the various states of emotional agitation in humans, it is important to pay special attention to animal reactivity, which is triggered by the emotional shock intended to avert a life-threatening situation. In order to be effective, primitive emotional reactivity can be only either *attack or flight* from danger. Observation will demonstrate the existence of a third form of response, inefficient in character, that is triggered in animals and humans alike when they are faced with a danger that is too suddenly perceived or too intense and insurmountable, so that neither of the safeguarding reactions of flight and attack are successfully triggered. Both reactions remain stuck in the body and their contradictory intentions produce a spasm that inhibits motivity. It is as if the escape and attack impulses, pulling in opposite directions, were mutually annihilating, paralyzing any reaction and thus creating a lethargic state. This convulsed form of a response to emotional shock results in the *reaction of surrender*. The innervation, instead of stimulating the motor apparatus, paradoxically discharges all its wrongly used energy into the neurovegetative system, which produces diffused and general somatic disorders such as shaking, palpitation, and perspiration.

These three *forms of organic-motor reactivity*—attack, escape, surrender—already correspond in the animal to three forms of *intrapsychic reactivity* (which is inevitably accompanied by organic disorder). *The characteristic of panic*, a feeling proper to psychic reactions, corresponds to the automatic characteristic common to the three somatic reactions to shock. *These three psychic reactions to an emotional shock are the panic fear (flight), the panic anger (attack), and the panic terror (surrender).*

In carnivores, the reaction of adaptation is infuriated attack. It is not triggered by the perception of mortal danger and, therefore, it is never transformed into a paroxysmal terror and surrender reaction.

Yet, the carnivores' attack also shows characteristic traits of emotional disturbance (organic disorder, tonic spasm, and panic nuance) because it is tied to the elementary survival need, which can be satisfied only through the discovery of the prey and the surprise attack. (It is interesting to verify that at the primitive level of life, even the reaction of fright and surrender is used for the aim of adaptation. Some insects become lethargic at the sign of danger. Little armed for escape, they better protect themselves by immobility, as a great many voracious animals recognize their prey by movement only.)

In humans, the reaction of surrender is pathological despair. But "paroxysmal fright" is the result of the inhibition of fearful escape as well as infuriated attack; escape and attack, with their psychic complementaries of fear and rage, are then left as the elementary reactions to the emotional shock.

At the human level, infuriated attack is anger. It is no longer a sign of strength, it is an indication of weakness. Powerless rage or resentment, the opposite of moral courage, is expressed by the term *wrath* (in French *courroux*, from *coeur* [heart] and *rompu* [ruptured], according to G. Paris).

Etymology stresses the genetic relation that starts with the elementary emotion of "rage" (physical courage) and leads to humanized feelings: *pathological rage* (anger or loss of self-control) and *moral courage* (the cogitated attack of intrapsychic cowardice, which is fear that has become anxiety). The elementary emotions of fear and rage become, in humans, either moral cowardice or moral courage by the intermediary of conscious foresight, a distinctive trait that distinguishes between the automatic reactivity of the animal psyche and the cogitative activity of the human psyche. Humans are not exposed to immediate mortal danger as much as they are to the multiple difficulties produced by the social environment. Because humans are capable of foreseeing difficulties, the escape and attack behavioral mechanisms are subjected to thought processes that can modify their value. Momentary withdrawal, a sign of poised patience, will often become a more valuable attitude and will prove greater courage than unconsidered attack.

The only one of the three elementary primitive reactions (attack, escape, surrender) that exists without modification in humans, is the fright and surrender reaction triggered by the sudden perception of a mortal and insurmountable danger, because it does not allow for the use of conscious foresight, or presence of mind. Yet the loss—at least partial—of presence of mind can occur at the human level when difficulties are confronted that are overexalted in the imagination yet are, in themselves, surmountable. The loss of presence of mind is then a sign of pathological regression and weakening of the psyche. Life-threatening aggression is usually excluded from interhuman rela-tionships, and the emotional agitations, fear and anger, even when provoked by actual threat, remain partially penetrated by an underly-ing thought that is often affectively blinded but still retains its inten-tional characteristic and thus *constitutes a calculating motivation.* Fear assumes an aspect of timidity, and anger becomes an attempt to intimidate. The fear-timidity is an attempt to ward off aggression by submissive retreat, while anger attempts, by exalted and disorganized threats, to intimidate and to provoke in the threatening adversary the reaction of surrender. These are affective states, halfway between the elementary emotion of instinctive life and the nuanced feelings that characterize humans. It is important not to confuse these affective feel-ings, often misadapted and pathological in humans, with the elemen-tary emotion of preconscious life.

*   *   *

This confusion is frequent, nonetheless, and has extremely serious con-sequences. It entails that classical psychology classify love, hate, or any affective function of the human psyche among elementary emo-tions. If Ribot adds tenderness, egoism, and sexuality to it, other authors will complete the classification, no less arbitrarily, by adding to it other humanized functions or feelings that have nothing in com-mon with elementary emotions except for the fact that they are their derived and differentiated nuances, and, therefore, they are life forms that, in the genetic hierarchy, have a completely different position from the elementary emotional phenomenon.

By far the most disastrous consequence is to confuse any coherent comprehension of the evolutionary genesis of psychic functioning. The absence of a preliminary study of elementary emotional reactivity, together with the ill-assorted combination of human affects (emotion-al agitations) taken as emotions, eventually masks the primordially important biogenetic phenomenon: the fearful flight and the infuriated attack, which, throughout prehuman evolution, create *the instincts of flight and attack,* diversified in numerous forms, each form essential-ly characterizing an animal species.

*   *   *

It is, however, of very secondary importance to determine whether an author committed errors while trying to establish the list of emotions. The essential point is to reveal the disastrous consequences of the lack of definitions.

It is not possible to determine the place occupied by human intra-psychic anxiety in relation to the elementary emotions of the animal without first situating animal emotivity in relation to its own biological substructure: the need for self-preservation and the drives, of which the instincts are the means of satisfaction.

* * *

1. The most elementary need, common to every living being, is to safeguard the psychophysical unity of the organism: *self-preservation*. The mistake is to speak of an instinct of self-preservation, which diminishes the elementarily irreducible results of the survival impulse, the energetic driving force of all life. Within it, all vital intensity suspended between joy of living and anxiety of death is condensed into a potentiality.

Instinct is merely one of the evolved means by which the living being will cling to existence and will adapt to the accidental conditions of survival. Evolution as a whole is only a specific manifestation of the elementary need for self-preservation.

Everything that works toward the satisfaction of the survival impulse will necessarily be experienced as a pleasure, and all that hinders it will be experienced as displeasure. (Often in classical psychology, pain is opposed to pleasure. This is reasonable only if one understands the term *pain* to mean psychic suffering or, more specifically, displeasure.) Pleasure and displeasure (*lust-unlust*) exist at the onset of the life of feelings; the most differentiated feelings of the human psyche remain impregnated with the "pleasure-displeasure" nuance. Yet, a complication of the feelings of pleasure and displeasure arises at the human level so it may seem incompatible with the simplicity of the proposed definition. To support the definition, it is essential to take this complication into consideration.

Already in animals, vital egoism or the need for self-preservation tends to expand ever further during the course of evolution and partly changes into the capacity to include into the individual's own pleasure the survival conditions of the sexual partner, the offspring, or even other members of the species. *The expansion of primitive egoism into lovingness becomes, in humans, a source of intensification of the vital pleasure called joy.* Thus a hierarchy is created among satisfactions, a *scale of values* that ranges from the lower pleasure of *self-love* (which is concerned only with the satisfaction of bodily needs) to the higher pleasure obtained through expanded egoism, which is sublimated into lovingness. Both sources of pleasure create a multitude of valiant feelings charged with value *in relation to the meaning of life, which is to prefer higher pleasures over lower pleasures, not because of an outer imposition, but uniquely due to the foreseeing egoism, which can recognize that in the shorter or longer term, the pleasure of lovingness leads to a more durable and intense satisfaction.*

An outcome of foreseeing egoism is to no longer consider only the safeguarding of one's own existence, but also the safeguarding of a meaningful orientation. The ethical value lies in the coherent egoism that entails loving the higher interest sufficiently not to experience it as an imposition foreign to nature. All human psychic distortions are attributable to the fact that humans subconsciously try to hide their vital insufficiency from themselves—their inability to expand egoism into love. Egoism does not succeed in detaching itself from the individual, but degrades into *egocentrism*. This perversion makes egoism *incoherent*. The individual believes himself to be the center of the world, which, in turn, seems to him to become more and more anxiety-laden and hostile because it opposes the satisfactions of his desires, which have become meaningless through exaltation. The transformational dynamism of anxiety (the displeasure that demands its transformation into pleasure) loses, thus, its positive force. Instead of preservation of psychic unity and union with others, there is a pathological dissociation. These functional complications that arise at the human level render difficult to comprehend the simple elementary relations among the need for satisfaction, pleasure and displeasure, and love and hate as they constitute the biopsychic foundation of all life.

*   *   *

2. It is important to distinguish *drives*, nutritional and sexual appetites, from the elementary need for egoistic self-preservation. The need for self-preservation materializes through drives; therefore it is through the drives that, in the course of evolution, the transformation of elementary egoism materializes into either love (expansion of the field of satisfactions) or egocentrism (restriction of the field of satisfactions).

From the start, the need for self-preservation manifests not only in the immediate sense of preservation (the defense of the organic unit against various dangers from the environment), but also in an expanding form. The living being is solicited by some excitations he prefers to others. He likes them. This first sign of love is not yet differentiated from the elementary egoism of preservation, which demands complete union, the incorporation of the favorite object; it possesses a characteristic of voracity. The elementary need, when expanding, manifests as hunger or an appetite that drives the being to seek satisfaction within the environment. Vital hunger is soon differentiated into two *elementary drives*: nutrition (preservation of the individual) and reproduction (preservation of the species).

Sexuality is gradually differentiated into an expanded lovingness, although this still remains a variation of elementary egoism in its most sublimated forms. *Sublimation of egoism into love is attained by a refinement of the demand for union that substitutes the psychic link of tenderness for voracious incorporation.* Voracity is indicated in that expression of tenderness, the kiss. The substitution of a psychic link for physical union already finds its most striking expression in animals, where the sexual drive manifests as the care of offspring. In this example, the elementary power of the egoistical need, as well as its tendency to sublimate into love, is verified. Everything happens as if the litter remained part of the mother's own need for self-preservation. The offspring remain, for the mother, a part of herself in spite of the differentiation of physical form. The substitutive link that is tender love seems so potent that the mother continues to defend the offspring as if she herself were being attacked; therefore, sublimated egoism or love can reverse the basic need for self-preservation into sacrifice of one's life.

Even the highest form of love, for humans, is a variation of coherent egoism, because it is the supreme result of healthy egoism to find the ultimate vital satisfaction in the joyful union with life, as a whole. *At the limit of the rarely attained sublime, coherent egoism is transformed into understanding and perfectly objective love: kindness.* Therefore, the primitive drive of voracious love is entirely transformed into the most subtle psychic link. *This total opening to life, the ultimate ideal of ego satisfaction, is the perfect opposite of the primitive closure of individualizing separation from which the elementary need for self-preservation began.*

Perverse reversal of egoism into egocentrism, the source of anxiety, is diametrically opposed to the sublime conversion of egoism into love, the source of joy. This ego expansion uses also, for its partial attainments, extraconscious paths (superconscious rather than subconscious), which are, too often, overlooked by the effort of psychological understanding. *Nothing impedes the coherent comprehension of the*

*genesis of psychic functioning more than the widespread prejudice that
establishes an irreducible opposition between love and egoism.*

* * *

3. It is important to distinguish *instincts* from the fundamental need
for self-preservation and the two elementary drives of nutrition and reproduction. A frequent source of confusion is the habit of labeling as
"instincts" all preconscious functions that are not yet well defined.
Nothing is more erroneous than to speak of self-preservation as an instinct or to classify sexuality as an instinct. The elementary need for
self-preservation and the drives are common to all species; instincts
differ, and these differences characterize each species.

Instincts are defined as a means to satisfy drives. The nutritional
drive in carnivores, for example, is satisfied by the instinct to hunt;
each grouping of carnivores is characterized by a different instinctive
way to proceed with the tracking, pursuit, and attack of prey. (At the
human level, instinctive reactivity becomes foreseeing activity. Nutrition and sexuality broaden into individualized needs and into a multitude of desires. Cogitation, which is still in part affective thought,
replaces instinctive automatism as the means of satisfaction. The motives of activity can be divided into two groups, lucid thought and affectively blinded motives. Lucid thought, often vainly, attempts to
control affectively blinded motives. This intrapsychic division generates conflicts, and along with them is intrapsychic anxiety.)

In animals, we can distinguish two forms of instinct: *elementary
instincts*, which concern immediate needs; and *secondary instincts*,
which contemplate future needs and are provided with some foresight.

The elementary instincts of hunting and flight are intimately tied
to stimulation through emotional shock (fear or rage, accompanied by
organic disturbances) because of the abruptness of the driving demand
they serve. This occurs not only with respect to the drive for nutrition;
in the sexual act, because of its characteristic of voracious tenderness,
defense and attack are inextricably tied with emotional nuances of
rage and fear. The inextricable mixing of these two elementary emotions determines the reaction of surrender in the female and the rage
of attack in the male. Unlike the nutritional drive, where survival is
truly at stake, the sexual act is attack mixed with tenderness and
flight, which became submission, and is reduced or heightened, as one
likes, to a superb play of life and death, a game of emotional excitation,
the deep meaning of which is triumph over death by the creation of a
new life.

The courage that incites attack and battle is, moreover, a form of emotivity so characteristic of the sexual drive that it also manifests in often fatal prelude games that are easily observable in certain species of birds and herbivores in which the males will battle fiercely for the female, but manifest the nutritional drive rather placidly.

Secondary instincts are derived in incalculable numbers from the elementary instincts of hunting and flight. In some species, especially in insects, secondary instincts attain a surprising degree of ingenuity and automatic foresight. The hunting instinct excels, for instance, in the construction of various traps. This same ingenuity can be found in the secondary instinct that serves the reproductive drive.

We can notice as well that the care given to offspring (especially in species lower than mammals) has the most varied secondary instincts. In the bird population, the instincts of nesting, which serve the care of offspring, are a differentiated product of the elementary instinct of escape (for instance, from unfavorable weather conditions). This posture of escape becomes predominant in migration instincts. Fear of bad weather or fear of the light of day can determine the flight instinct in the most ferocious mammals, and can force them to take refuge in their resting places. Gregarious instincts, in their primitive form, can derive from hunting instincts, (as they do, for instance, with wolves), but they proceed more often from the escape instinct. The gregarious instinct is also more common to herbivores, who do not have to fight over prey and who search together for food and security. It is as if fear drives them to huddle together as a flock, where they are assured of more security.

Secondary instincts, with the common characteristic of automatic foresight as a trait, can be considered a foreshadowing of the conscious vigilance that characterizes humans. This intermediary result can be established equally on the affective level. Unlike the elementary instincts of hunting and flight, the derived instincts no longer concern the sudden appearance of an actual threat. The emotional nuance accompanying them no longer shows the spasmodic characteristic of shock. *Disturbances in organic functions and panic of the psychic functioning manifest in a lighter and scattered way, which favors the differentiation of elementary emotivity into a multiform affectivity.* The emotivity, particularly in higher animals, begins to bring nuance into various emotional agitations, foreshadowing the wealth of the feeling life that characterizes the human being.

* * *

The preceding sketch establishes with only very broad strokes a comprehensive view of the genesis of psychic functioning. However, it hints at the possibility that *evolution might not only concern the soma but that it could also be a phenomenon of a psychic order*. Biology studies evolution only from the outside and looks for the principle of evolutionary adaptation in the outside world, finding it, for example, in the fight for survival. From the perspective of psychological study, the principle of evolution that is intrapsychic in nature lies, in the transformational dynamism of anxiety. Moreover, it is clear that there is a correlation between those two principles, as the fight for survival is the outer condition of psychic anxiety. None of the biological theories can explain all the wealth of detail in the adaptive process and extract from it a principle of orientation, a directive hypothesis, able to open a perspective that embraces all facets of the problem. This state of affairs is not denied, but, on the contrary, strongly emphasized by some of the most intelligent biologists, such as J. Rostand.

Such a restriction imposes itself in respect to Pavlov's physiological theory of evolution. The outer conditioning would not have any hold on a body-matter deprived of excitability. In order for the excitability, which is the seed of the psyche, to be capable of evolving to the lucidity of spirit, the spirit must already be latently present. The "seed" of spirit that can be revealed in excitability constitutes the "conditionability" that precedes conditioning. It is irritability, fundamental restlessness or anxiety in its most elementary form. Elementary anxiety is nascent spirit, for it bears in itself the need to be overcome. This demand is the elementary need for self-preservation and satisfaction. The satisfying self-preservation can be accomplished only by way of evolutionary adaptation, which occurs in these stages: the elementary need to survive, drives, instinctive automatism, emotions, diversified affectivity, affective thought, and lucid thought. Without the original existence of this primary psychic quality, the seed of spirit that is conditionability, irritability, and fundamental restlessness—the distinctive trait between inanimate matter and living soma—evolution could not be accomplished. In the same way, the organic differentiation that is concentrated in the elaboration of the nervous system and that culminates in cerebration, the organic equivalent of psychic lucidity, could not be accomplished without the material substratum or without the original existence of an undifferentiated cell. *Somatic evolution and psychic evolution go together;* they constitute two inseparable aspects of the evolution of the psychosomatic organism.

The brain is only the somatic condition of thought. No confusion could be more disastrous than to pretend to demonstrate the birth of thought by contenting oneself to study the stages of cerebration. It is very useful, for instance, to establish experimentally the close correspondence between affectivity and thought, and subcortical and cortical centers. However, the existence of such a correspondence is far from proof that the psyche is only an epiphenomenon of the organic. Pavlov has emphasized on several occasions that his theory is only a physiology of evolution, leaving a clear field to psychological study.

*   *   *

Like the preference for the study of organic disorders, giving significance only to the outer conditioning and neglecting inner conditionability is caused by the idea that the outer, more readily observable, can provide the object of research. We must establish even more firmly the basis for the study of intrapsychic anxiety and demonstrate that to follow the slant of the organicist tendency is risking failure to recognize the meaning of evolution.

The evolutionary goal is not to make living beings independent of outer conditioning, which would be impossible, but to free them as far as possible from outside determination. The entire problem of intrapsychic anxiety could be defined by this evolutionary goal, since intimate anxiety is the measure of the failure of the effort to achieve freedom.

Instinct passively adapts the animal to the conditions of the environment, which, in turn, condition the animal completely. In humans, this primitive situation is reversed. The human species, due to the ingenuousness of the intellect, attempts to adapt the outer world to its needs. Only one condition is likely to cause the failure of this active adaptation; it is intrapsychic in nature, and it is the possibility of multiplying and exalting needs to an unattainable extent. Lucid control—a supreme intrapsychic quality—should actively condition the outer world according to necessity *and also be devoted to fighting the tendency to exalt those needs*, the cause of inner disorder and the intimate source of anxiety.

The two domains of lucid control determine two very distinct intrapsychic functions: *the utilitarian intellect*, directed toward the outer world in order to satisfy any need; and *the spirit* (restraining of reason), which is fit to valuate the multiple needs in order to prevent their exaltation. The spirit, therefore, more decisively than the intellect, liberates an individual from outer conditioning. Conditioned by the intellectual effort of the now conscious species, the social milieu be-

comes a conditioning factor for each individual insofar as the autonomous conditioning of the subject, which is the spiritual control of affectivity, is inadequate. Humans stay passively conditioned by the outside
environment as much as by inner anxiety insofar as they are unsuc-
cessful in causing in and by themselves the evolutionary reversal of
passive conditioning into active liberating conditionability. The highest degree of this evolution is the liberating spiritualization that transforms the primary egoism into "lovingness."

A psychic science based only on the study of outer conditioning
may fail to recognize the true psychological problem: internalized conditioning or motivation in two diametrically opposed forms that determine the intrapsychic conflict: *affective disorientation, the source of
anxiety; and lucid orientation, the source of rejoicing satisfaction.*

This reversal of outer conditioning—into inner motivations—
relates to the other evolutionary reversal already ascertained: the
reversal of elementary egoism *into either pathological egocentrism or
coherent egoism (the foresight of which envisions, in the highest interest of the ego, reversal of egocentrism and its blossoming into love of
life).* The connection between those two forms of reversal—and even
their identity—is an unavoidable consequence of evolution toward a
greater lucidity. The reversal of passive conditioning by the environment into motivating self-conditionability can be accomplished only
after an internalization of a still more general nature that generates
the human psyche and its half-conscious lucidity. All objects are reflected in the psyche and leave their imprint, which creates the representative image of the world. The affective imagination and the cognitive representation determine the functioning of the human psyche,
now half-conscious. Through the conflict of these two opposing functions all the psychic work is accomplished—either exaltation of anxiety or its assuagement, which is *the intrapsychic conditioning of the
essential destiny of an individual.*

* * *

To the accidental outer conditioning is then added the essential conditioning by inner-represented objects *in the form of either images
charged with blind affectivity or concepts full of lucid objectivity.* The
work of objectivation, of liberation from the subjugating ascendancy of
the outer world (in regard to outer conditioning) can be accomplished
only at the level of intrapsychic representation. Objects that are internalized and stabilized in a representation can now be submitted to a
cognitive and conceptualizing comparison, from which (by the inter-

mediary of language, which fixes the significance and extent of concepts) intellectual and utilitarian thought will emerge. A yet more evolutionary form of thought will also emerge—the foreseeing mind, the function of which is orientation toward the evolutionary meaning of life due to the valuation of represented objects. The guiding ideal of the valuating mind will be the highest interest of an individual—the realization of coherent egoism aspiring to a meaningful satisfaction.

The mind, by its value judgment concerning future satisfaction, tends to guarantee orientation in time. It thus shows its incorporation in an evolutionary continuum, which links it to the ability of orientation in space from a distance, an ability already secured by animals through sensory apparatus. Just as the animal is distinct from plant life, rooted in the soil, by the necessity to move in space and the sensory ability to orient itself while in search of outwardly conditioned vital satisfaction, humans are distinct from animals *in the possibility of going astray* in the maze of internalized conditioning, and also *in the ability to orient themselves by internalized sight or introspection, a form of spiritual prevision.*

The evolutionary organization of the soma, on the other hand, remains subjected to the demand of localizing the means of transport (the limbs), the organs of drives (especially the digestive tract, which decides the form of the trunk), and the sensory organs, the genuine tentacles and antennae of the brain (which result in modeling the head and the face). The organization of the body is perfected in higher animals, where the upright position and the liberation of the hand are already marked; along with it there is a spark of intelligence. The most evolved animal species, however, is first characterized by the predominance of sensory and spatial orientation and the automatic rigidity of instinctive foresight. Both are perfectly adapted to the passive conditionability that depends entirely upon the environment.

Starting with the human species, a *decisive mutation* is taking place without any interruption in the evolutionary continuum. The somatic organization, which was until now strikingly predominant as an adaptive means, gives way to the decisive differentiation of the intrapsyche, which escapes outside observation. This is where the mentioned upheavals intervene: the representative internalization of the perceived world and the evolutionary demand of an introspective control and organization of the accentuated complexity of the intrapsyche. Negligence in regard to this immanent demand generates *human anxiety, specifically the feeling of guilt, the result of an ultimate differentiation of vital restlessness.* The genetic cause of this differentiation, its essential conditioning, is the manifestation of psychic disorder, which occurs as a consequence of the multiplication of desires. Purely an inner phenomenon, the guilty anxiety is no longer primarily conditioned from outside. *Repression of guilty anxiety will generate a procession of involutionary complications that become the pathological functioning of the human psyche.*

In order to complete this preliminary outline of the genesis of intrapsychic anxiety, it is appropriate to quote Pradines's (1946) book, *Traité de psychologie generale.* Although envisioned from another angle and developed entirely differently, there is a theory of evolution that, in many ways, agrees with the concepts just proposed. The most important point of comparison is the idea that the spirit is not a psychic function that emerges—nobody knows just where from—inexplicably and almost supernaturally in the course of evolution, but that it is already foreshadowed, even in a still preconscious form, in the most elementary functioning of the psychophysical organism, indicating that evolutionary adaptation has no other aim than to unfold the *immanent "seed" of the spirit.* It is very satisfying to note that research pursued along similar lines leads to converging perspectives.

B. ANXIETY IN THE THEORY OF DUMAS AND JANET

With the intention of tying as securely as possible the study of the psyche to the method of exact sciences, Dumas neglects to an extreme degree the study of the intrapsyche and pays attention only to the organic disorder, which he attempts to render measurable by graphic diagrams.

Since, in the human psyche, the life of feelings underlies not only the will (by codetermining hesitations and decisions) but also thought (restlessness of doubt and joy of knowledge), Dumas pretends that he submitted the entire psyche to quantitative mensuration, while contenting himself to measure and represent only the vascular and respiratory disorder of some affective states with graphic diagrams.

By completing graphic diagrams with an abundant study of the mimic expression of feelings-emotions, Dumas succeeds in writing a book titled *La vie affective* (1948), which is certainly very rich in insights of all kinds and often very interesting, but rigorously excludes the study of the intrapsyche with the pretext that feelings that are intimately experienced are only an ideo-affective agitation lacking significance. However, this is how Dumas defines emotion: "motion or cessation of motion, changes in organic life and a *sui generis* state of consciousness" (p. 85). As a result of this definition and in order to analyze emotivity, one would have to study not only the organic disorder but also the state of consciousness.

Dumas relates the following observation among many examples of a similar kind that he quotes in support of his utmost organicity: "As soon as a slight incident has occurred around her, a call, a sentence she has heard or the simple fact that I am getting close to her bed, she starts 'evoking' and immediately, reacting to the evoked representations, she screams, moans and groans, knots and twists her hands, her heart beats faster and her pressure gets higher" (p. 94). Later, he adds: "If one could make this ideo-affective agitation disappear by puffing it away, Augustine would not be cured, she would remain depressed and anxious; and when she got agitated or excited, she would add her depression to the agitation of a depressed and weak person" (p. 95). For Dumas, this case would be an example of the emotive state he calls "active sadness."

The distinction between sadness (a feeling rather than an emotion) and melancholy (the morbid exaltation of this feeling) is so usual in psychiatry that there is every reason to think that Dumas neglects it for his own reasons. He does not go so far as to pretend that the cause of ideo-affective agitation is the physical agitation, the knotting and twisting of the hands, but he certainly is not far from thinking that it lies in the acceleration of the heartbeat and in the blood pressure. In any case, he suggests that the genuine cause of the psychic disorder is to be found in the "agitation of a depressed and weak person," that is to say, according to Dumas, in organic weakness. It certainly plays a part, but there are a number of cases of organic weakness that do not produce any psychic depression. The description of the case demonstrates precisely that which outwardly conditions depressive exaltation—the slight incidents—would remain inoperative if an intrapsychic cause were not added as well: the evocation of representations.

The idea that a light puff of breath is sufficient to remove this intrapsychic cause testifies to a prejudice that belittles its importance. It doesn't suffice to breathe on this ideo-affective agitation for it to evaporate: its nature is obsessing and its source is subconscious.

Morbid anxiety, accumulated subconsciously, supplies reactivity with excessive convulsive energy and provokes psychic as well as somatic agitation. If we troubled to study the nature of this anxiety and the cause of its accumulation, instead of claiming that a slight puff of breath would disperse it, we could perhaps succeed in quieting not only the evocational exaltation but also the agitation of the hands, the acceleration of the heartbeat, and other organic symptoms.

The reason Dumas gives for his contempt of ideo-affective agitation is the manifestation of apparent monotony in melancholic subjects. In cases of pathological euphoria in which he calls manic patients the "joyful subjects" (in order to justify his intention to use mania for his graphic study of joy), Dumas declares that "their ideas are not poor nor monotonous but varied and rich" (p. 101). This by no means leads him to analyze the wealth of intrapsychic data, although on this occasion he makes a remark perhaps betraying that he does not deny the need for such analysis, but renounces the pursuit of it in detail on account of its so-called ease. After his observation of the difference in the ideation of melancholiacs and joyfuls, he adds, "The feelings and the intellectual characteristics are such that it is easy to discern them in the joyfuls and in oneself when one analyzes active joy" (p. 101). It is, moreover, very strange to see in Dumas's theory an allusion to intimate observation contained in these lines.

We can say, in general, that extreme organicism comes from the fact that morbid feelings, in Dumas's theory, simply become emotions. This is especially noticeable with the feeling of "anxiety" that Ribot— as we saw—has already tried to distinguish from the emotion of "fear." Dumas agrees to the definition (proposed by James Sully, 1904) according to which fear would be "the emotional reaction caused by vivid and persistent representation of possible pain or ill" (p. 105)—*a definition that corresponds more to anxiety*, as its distinctive characteristic is *to envision future and possible evil,* and has, by the same token, underlying vivid representations, like all feelings, *while fear is the emotional response to an actual trauma that is provoked by a real danger.* (Confusion, viewed as a definition, is eliminated but still characterizes classical psychiatry.) Dumas ceaselessly quotes cases of anxiety with the intention to provide examples of fear, and everywhere in the explanatory text, the terms *fear* and *anxiety* are synonyms.

It will be very obvious that apparent objectivity is likely to disguise a profound subjectivity that causes a great deal of imprecision. The root of this subjectivity lies in the tendency to neglect the study of the intrapsyche, which is contemptuously called "ideo-affective agitation." What could be more dangerously confusing, in the human sciences and in therapy, than to eliminate objectivity from research under the pretext that the term *objective* means "observation of somatic manifestations" to the exclusion of the phenomenon of study, which should be ideo-affective agitation. Impartiality toward this intrapsychic phenomenon is certainly difficult, but, as we will see, it is not impossible.

It is bewildering to see such great and talented minds such as Dumas and especially Ribot becoming lost. They are characterized by an exceptional acuteness of penetration that is exerted, however, in a misguided direction, resulting in the extent of the final misconception. The best hiker cannot arrive at his destination if he persists in deviating from the only path that could take him there.

*   *   *

In order to gain insight into the conditions of the genesis of human anxiety, it is important to insist further on the clear distinction between elementary emotivity and the affective life of feelings, too often a cause of psychic illnesses.

No affective couple such as sadness and joyfulness can or should be placed on the same level as the elementarily emotional couple: fear and anger (flight and attack). On the conscious level, fear and anger no longer concern (except the appearance of a sudden peril) life-threatening danger, but concern rather the multiplicity of obstacles, as opposed to the realization of multiple desires. Far from being part of elementary emotions, fear and anger become, in humans, feelings of multiple nuances, that is to say, affective states that are likely to extend imaginatively into the past and future. Imaginative fear is anxiety. Reactivity is no longer immediate and automatic; it has underlying intentions, anxiety-laden motives that, triggered by threat, foresee—by way of imaginative exaltation—the difficulty, if not the impossibility, of a future and adequate release.

For the animal, the emotions of fear and anger are triggered by an actual threat and are clearly distinct by their tonality of either courage or cowardice. *But emotions, while they become intentional and semiforeseen feelings in humans, ceasing to be elementary, separate from the real and present object and become fixed to the representative image of the object and the affective foresight of the threat.* All emotions, hence sentimental affections, form a vaguely intentional imagination where the images of foreseen threats linger. Through the imaginative faculty, the multiple affective nuances (the tonalities of courage and cowardice, inspired by any given obstacle) are now exposed to an intense *intrapsychic* work that can rectify cowardice or dishearten courage. Correction or disheartening depends upon the degree of lucidnity—affective or blindness—of the semiforeseeing imagination. *The blindness to which the imagination remains subject, should morbid exaltation occur, is the residue of the panic mechanism of elementary emotivity.*

Insofar as its intention is a panic aggression, anger itself becomes cowardice. In the event foresight remains blinded, a kind of fusion between fear and anger—but not sufficiently elucidated—results from the intrapsychic work that is now possible at the level of half-foreseeing imagination. In that manner, a kind of absorption of courage by cowardice takes place, an imaginative intimidation that is the source of intrapsychic anxiety in its morbid aspect. Even though fused into a single feeling of anxiety, fear and anger and their respective tendencies, flight and attack, are still visible within morbid anxiety. They determine the two *ambivalent* traits that characterize it: inhibition and aggression. Therefore, multiple-formed intrapsychic anxietude (worry, resentment, shyness, and so on) originates in the half-conscious psyche, from elementary emotivity. Although each feeling of anxiety is accidentally triggered by surrounding conditions, the cause of the anxious state is essentially intimate in nature. Anxietude results from *an insufficient intrapsychic work*; if the intrapsychic work occurs properly, it ought to be capable of mastering the influx of excitations. Failing to master excitations brings about exalted anxiety, which is likely to reach pathological degrees (justifying the term *anxietude*).

Imputable to imaginative rumination and its blinding power, morbidity exists in the lack of "presence of mind" that produces the insufficient elucidation of a danger, henceforth a represented and anxiety-laden obstacle. *"Presence of mind," the highest adaptive quality, is the opposite of primitiveness of panic automatism.* In fact, the adaptive goal of the imaginative internalization of an exciting danger is the rupture of the panic automatism. In the internalization, the represented danger should undergo foreseeing cognition rather than rumination. Due to this meaningful reestablishment, the primitively perturbing danger should be viewed as a problem to be solved. Insofar as this evolutionary possibility is actualized, the represented danger and the negative feelings nuanced by discouragement, cowardice, and anxiety in turn undergo a spiritually valuating control. "Anxietude" is thus submitted to revision by a form of courage that is no longer primitive in nature but of an intrapsychic and ethical order. From this spiritualizing revision of intrapsychic anxiety, the scale of positive feelings comes into being, valorous because spirited, encouraging, and rejoicing. Opposed to intrapsychic anxiety in its multiple forms, characterized by the powerless rage that turns them into hate, is the joy of spiritual accomplishment with its multiple forms, which is characterized by the power of ethical courage, an attitude free from all panic-stricken bewilderment, and that engenders benevolence rather than hate.

Therefore, in a genetic perspective, sadness is not opposed to joy, as Dumas would think. *The positive complementary of sadness is gaiety. Joy is the positive complementary of anxiety.* Sadness and gaiety are feelings due to the propensity of temperament and are randomly triggered by outer events. *Anxiety and joy,* on the other hand, *are durable states of being. They indicate the vital value or nonvalue of the individual, for they are essentially consequential to the positive or negative nature of intrapsychic work.*

The distinctions established give us an insight into the total arbitrariness of the attempt to base the psychology of affectivity on the mensuration of anxiety that is morbid to a psychotic degree. Primarily, they demonstrate all the pathogenic power of ideo-affective agitation. To complete this analysis, we must demonstrate that the psychogenetic definitions established so far help us to understand the *common* and *differentiating features* that exist between commonly experienced anxiety and the psychotic state.

At a lesser degree of morbid anxietude, at the level of simple nervousness, imagination already ceaselessly evokes a multitude of means of defense or attack, in the attempt to ward off threats (viewed as emerging from all sides). The result of anxiety-laden disorientation, these ragingly exalted or fearfully inhibited means of attack or defense no longer conform to the demands of reality, and their incoherent discharge leads to failure reactions. The confusion increases. Whenever the hereditary ground lends itself to the situation and the hostility of reality is insurmountable, morbid anxiety risks being aggravated into a permanent terror characterized by the panic reaction of surrender, which manifests in the imagination as a despair toward life similar to *the lethargic and panic state of primitive beings' fear when confronted with a life-threatening danger.*

Motor lethargy (catatonia) and panic frenzy (imaginative delusion) appear and crown the reaction of surrender that characterizes the psychotic stage of morbid anxietude. The now delirious ideo-affective agitation is ceaselessly preoccupied with vital threats, ceaselessly ruminates represented dangers and suggests illogical means to flee or attack. The imagination "hallucinates" unreal dangers and wanders astray into desperate flights. It has, moreover, the power to depict a successful attack fallaciously and thus succeeds in engendering a pathological euphoria, a delusion of hope and even victory that, still pervaded with exasperated anxiety, is caricatured as absurd thoughtlessness or grotesque gaiety (Dumas's "joyous subjects").

These two psychotic states, mania and melancholy, often alternate in the same patient, which is proof of their common root. (These reversed states are coupled with a deceleration or an exacerbation of vegetative functions. It is difficult to understand the organic cause of these often very sudden reversals, which cause melancholy to topple over into euphoric mania and vice versa. Should not psychic causation—their common root—with the influence it exerts on the soma, especially on glandular function, provide the explanation for these alternations?) What error could be greater than to confuse sadness with melancholic despair, and to take, furthermore, euphoric mania as an experimental base, with the pretext of so measuring liberating joy? The measure of joy is the degree of liberation from anxiety, and this degree cannot be known by mensuration but only by the analysis of the intrapsyche.

Moreover, this sort of mensuration has long been dismissed; this does not preclude that it is interesting to see where the desire to consider anxiety exclusively in its organic aspect erroneously led. Nevertheless, to assert that the indispensable study of peripheral manifestations obtained only questionable results would be prejudice. Psychiatry, in a theoretical rather than therapeutic aim, subjected all disorders—whether nervous, glandular, vascular, tonic, or motor—to investigation. If, by fear of being prompted into a domain it judges subjective, psychiatry generally recoils from the task of providing a genetic explanation for anxiety in its intimate form, it is certainly impressed by the ideo-affective disorders of delusion and hallucinations. At least, it established a description and a classification of syndromes.

Dumas was a more remarkable psychiatrist than psychologist. In a study called "Le supernaturel et les dieux d'apres les maladies mentales," he writes:

> The patients would have the feeling of an energy imposing upon them, fighting them; they would become anxious to fight it. Would they not be tempted, at times, to attribute a supernatural character, divine or demonic to this force, depending on their beliefs and state of mind? Expecting little precision or certitude because of their psychosis, can we accept the idea that they move toward the supernatural in this manner? That is to say, by their awareness of the opposition between their obsessions and their will? (Dumas, 1946, p. 163)

Dumas, in this and many other quotes, gives such significance to ideo-affective agitation that it becomes difficult to understand the contempt he affects toward it in *La vie affective*. What would be the cause of the conflict between obsession and will if not intrapsychic anxiety? And if it is useless to expect precision and certitude from the patients about this conflict, is it not justified to hope that the psychiatrist or the psychologist would successfully shed light on the nature of this conflict—the essential cause of mental illness—or fail the mission of both the therapist and the scientist?

* * *

In psychiatry in general, the most enigmatic problem remains the striking disorder of the mental functions, particularly in functional psychosis, where organic causes are so barely discernible that it is difficult not to admit causation of an intimate order. This problem eventually compelled psychiatric research to advance beyond the stage of description and classification of delusional states.

The French school opened the way to the study of the extraconscious functioning of the psyche. Bernheim, Charcot, and Janet, among others, prepared the way for the in-depth study of the intimately experienced aspect of anxiety. Therefore, examining the concept of anxiety in Janet's theory as it is summarized in the beginning of the second part of his main work *De l'angoisse a l'extase* (1926) will be useful. The present critique doesn't permit paying all the honor due to this very significant author. The concern for conciseness in this present work constrains us to overlook the positive contribution of Janet's work.

Janet, rebellious toward purely organicist theories, distinguishes himself from his predecessors by being the first to envision openly the problem of anxiety without being restricted to the study of outer conditioning and organic response. If he attempts to emphasize the significance of inner conditionability, he does not, however, succeed in breaking completely free from the well-known tendency to minimize. Janet introduces here the term *conduct*[1], which takes into account a kind of merging of the two elements that determine the activity: the intrapsychic cause and the observable effects (the reactions, organic as well as motor).

The terminological fusion is likely to bring about confusion. While accepting intimate causation, it allows the significance to shift to behavioral conduct and eventually studies only the outwardly observable reactions of the psychosomatic organism. All of Janet's work tends to admit and deny the significance of intimate functioning simultaneously. Janet looks for the causes of morbid anxiety in the sudden halt of orderly activity and in the resulting failure reactions.

This cessation could not provoke the continual attitude of failure in humans if it were not producing a kind of permanent cessation in the intrapsyche, following the anxiety-laden representation of unreal and imaginatively exalted dangers. The cessation of the activity and the resulting multiple failures are merely the effect of the intrapsychic transformation of past emotional agitations into anxious rumination (resentment, vexation, the need for revenge, intimidation, and so on). Janet considers the behavior of fear, manifest timidity, to be the cause of anxietude, believing he has explained intrapsychic phenomenon from behavior. He is, in fact, reversing the chain of cause and effect.

Janet, moreover, admits implicitly that his definition of anxiety, which concerns only accidental failure, is inadequate since he completes it with another definition that, while envisioning the intrapsychic "object," the essential cause of anxiety, attempts to deny its existence. According to Janet's definition, anxiety would be "a fear without object." It is correct to say that anxiety is *a temporally extended fear* that no longer concerns a present object, but rather concerns the imaginative representation of the object-obstacle. *For anxiety, the entire situation (not only the feeling toward the obstacle, but the object itself) is then concentrated in the intrapsyche.*

Contact with the anxiety-laden situation is actually and forever lost—we could be entitled to affirm that anxiety is without any real object—when the anxiety-laden representation of the object is inadequate, or when it is illusory imagination. Removed from its object and in this way disoriented, morbid anxiety fluctuates and is likely to cling imaginatively to any other object. This pathological transformation can be due only to an unhealthy ideo-affective agitation that became a habit. The genuine object of morbid anxiety is not outside, it is *psychic deficiency.*

It seems that the meaning of the term *intrapsychic anxiety* is now clear enough. Anxiety is intrapsychic because its represented or imagined object is affectively internalized and mainly because, when it is morbid, it is generated by the unhealthy constellation of the psyche, independently from the outer situation.

*   *   *

Anxiety appears to be without an object when one persists in trying to find its object exclusively in the extrapsychic (the organic and the surroundings). The intrapsychic danger is the most essential peril of life. It decides the involutionary distortion of the psyche that can extend to the onirically disguised explosion of anxiety, the cause of psychopathic symptoms.

However, repressing anxiety manifests in lesser degrees in the secret intimacy of all humans. Repressed, anxiety becomes timid or aggressive. It creates false motivations and false self-justifications, causing excessive accusation of others. All social and individual life, all actions and interactions are insidiously distorted by the misdeeds of repressed anxiety.

To expose repressed anxiety requires an entire elucidating endeavor, a fight of lucid mind against blinding affect. It is for this reason that intrapsychic anxiety easily becomes *anxiety of the intrapsychic problem*—the most characteristic feature of classical psychology. This anxiety that, under the pretext of objectivity, claims the intimate problem to be without object, provokes a "reaction of cessation." The situation of failure in psychology is certainly not the cause of the phobia of the intimate problem, but its effect. The cause is the vertigo that grabs anyone who approaches the depth of the extraconscious, considered unfathomable. Are we facing a kind of panicked emotional agitation that is not without recalling a very primitive reaction of fear and surrender? Nevertheless, the subconsciously determined surrender is opposed by the transformational dynamism in its positive form. The problem of intrapsychic anxiety leads to the discovery of the extraconscious.

C. Anxiety in Psychoanalysis

The psyche is a set of more or less conscious functions. The extraconscious is distinct from the conscious by the illogicality of its expressions, which are composed, as a whole, of the unreality of daydreams, the onirism of psychopathic symptoms (extending to delusional and hallucinatory dreams), dreams and collective dreams or mythologies.

All of these extraconscious expressions contain underlying meanings that are symbolically veiled; they concern subconsciously accumulated anxiety, or the more-than-conscious effort to overcome obsessive anxiety. The subconscious symbology of psychopathic symptoms is a caricature of mythical symbolism that is a superconscious expression of the immanent meaning of life and, therefore, the very foundation of our culture. (As mentioned earlier, Dumas, very opposed even to envisioning an underlying meaning of delusions, was tempted to connect the ideo-affective agitation of the patients with mythical symbology, which is an expression of religious feeling—as distinct from religion.)

The historical fact is that the symbolism of myths created numerous religions that have the same goal: to dam the collective overflow of anxiety. These facts indeed show that the symbolism of the superconscious must be preoccupied, according to its hidden meaning, with the most important problem of life: anxiety and the means to free oneself from it or, similarly, to transform it into joy. Consequently, psychology, by trying to penetrate the problem of anxiety to its extraconscious roots, must encounter mythical symbolism and the problem of its hidden meaning.

Nevertheless, the task of psychology has been singularly simplified because, to avoid compromising its method, it was necessary to neglect the study of extraconscious functioning. Is not this apparent simplification the source of all the complications? Does it not confine psychology within a dilemma that conveys its untenable position? Either the extraconscious does not exist—and then it would suffice to inspect the psyche (exposed to the conscious) in order to describe all its functioning—or the extraconscious is a psychic *reality* and must then be considered as an object of study. It is perhaps the only "object" that requires a thorough enough effort of analysis to grasp its hidden content.

In fact, this dilemma determines the actual situation in psychology. Part of the research remains attached to the old ideal of objectivity that professes salvation in the exclusive study of the organic while some schools are inclined to explore the intrapsychic and even the extraconscious; but in so doing, they incur the reproach of becoming lost in excessive subjective speculations. The reproach is justified because the effort of penetration has ceased halfway. The point of the endeavor is to propose a new "object" of research, the intrapsyche, and to use the familiar method of outer observation to explore it. I do not say that clinical observation is useless. Far from it. I am emphasizing the obvious fact that all manifestations of the human psyche remain analogically tied and that the psychological interpretation of morbid phenomena is possible only because it can be analogically reduced to anxiety-laden disorders that are observable in a normal psyche. Once the extraconscious is acknowledged and the nature of its entanglement with the conscious is established, the apparently considerable divergence between the normal expressions and the onirical distortions of anxiety loses its enigmatic aspect. As long as psychology did not take the extraconscious into account, it denied the existence of the sequence that led from the norm to onirism. This denial still is, in fact, frequent in psychiatry. Janet was first to admit the extraconscious functioning, and the title of his great work *De l'angoisse a l'extase* (ecstasy in the sense of mystical delusion) indicates his innovative aim to expose the link between anxiety and delusion.

Freud, in particular, oriented psychological psychiatry in a new direction. He discovered the symbolic expression of the subconscious that permits one to understand, from repressed anxiety, the meaning and pathogenesis of neurotic and schizophrenic symptoms. Freud thus opened the door to the analytical interpretation of the striking disturbances that are clinically observable. The interpretation reintroduces a speculative element into psychology that is liable to invade psychiatry as well.

In this respect, it is important to recall that classical organicism, on the whole, is merely a reaction against an old form of speculative interpretation that regarded the mentally ill patient as being actually possessed by an unhealthy spirit, the punishing demon. The spiritualist exaltation of this thesis provoked the organicist exaltation of the antithesis and, in short, Freud proposed a synthesis by demonstrating that the unhealthy spirit is not a demon that possesses the patient, but an anxiety that obsesses him. Thus, an intrapsychic principle was established that is opposed to exclusive organicism as well as to superstitious spiritualism, while it attempts to retain what is valuable in both. The Freudian perspective allows one to understand that the "demon" is only a symbolic personification of the real intrapsychic phenomenon, the unhealthy mind or repressive anxiety.

Once the intrapsychic principle is acknowledged, the principal concern should be to define it as clearly as possible; this can be accomplished only by clearly distinguishing it from the organic factor, which is by no means less active. The intrapsychic interpretation of anxiety does not oppose the organic interpretation, provided the two forms of interpretation are sufficiently objective to delineate, respectively, their domain and their method of work. Each of these two methods of explanation should begin with prepathological anxiety as it is normally manifested in the life of every human (and also, as anxiety is a specific form of fear, in the life of every living being).

The indications and causes of prepathological anxiety are rather monotonous. It is an entirely different matter for morbid anxiety and its repressive power. However, the analogical bridge still persists. In one of his books, *Psychopathology of Everyday Life*, Freud (1914) demonstrates that some reactions of the normal person—omission, linguistic lapses, failed reactions—are symbolically significant manifesta tions. This usual output of the psyche can be explained as a suffusion of semirepressed anxiety, but it does not extend beyond the imaginative level and does not reach the deeper strata of the subconscious. It is a process of false justifications that occurs very frequently and grafts pseudosublime pretext motives onto the motives of prohibited actions that are often shameful and painful to admit.

Freud was content to draw attention to the phenomenon he called "false rationalization." Instead of tying his analytical attention to this first sign of actually existing repression, he based his theory on the restrospective study of complexes. Even if we admit that complexes exist in an exclusively sexual form, as Freud claims, does not the spirit of scientific accuracy demand the analysis of every complex phenomenon, rather than taking it as a principle of explanation? According to Freud, the patient's infantile complexes are the residue of trauma due to the family background. But where would the pathological dynamism of these complexes come from, if they were not compounded motives of action that had been removed from conscious control since childhood and have now become subconscious? To exert a pathogenic influence, these motives, which have been welded into complexes, must have been affectively distorted, and, because they were formed during childhood before the growth of the reasoning function, they are irrational and illogical, possessing an indissoluble complexity. Persistent complexes become the cause of the distortion of adult psyches. Because these affective complexes already contained the pathogenic principle— wrong motivation—even in childhood, they still predetermine, after the ontogenic awakening of reasoning, its falsely justifying use, wrong rationalization that is already excessively used by the child. The true cause of adult psychopathy is not past trauma, but the fact that the reasoning remains childish and serves only to justify egocentrism that is the residue of undisciplined childhood.

If Freud had applied himself to analyzing wrong rationalization systematically, he would necessarily have discovered that wrong motivation—the stratagem of repressive anxiety—should be attacked during the healing analysis to render the adult capable of objective reasoning in relation to the world and to himself as well. Indeed, the patient heals as he learns to introspect objectively. In this respect, let us recall that Karen Horney, who came from a Freudian school, attempted, alone but courageously, to introduce within Freudianism introspective analysis (see Horney, 1942). This was a remarkable attempt, although laborious, because she relied heavily on the use of associations (the true source of arbitrary interpretation).

Freud himself was far from denying the possibility of self-observation. *He must have used it to discover the intimately hidden exist-*

ence of a wrong rationalization. He could have avoided the speculative interpretation of intimate functioning only if he had developed the necessary self-observation into an acknowledged method. Is there a more efficient process of objectification than the process that successfully accepts the *very principle of nonbjectivity: the principle of misuse of reasoning* or wrong motivation? To gain perspective on the distorting importance of wrong motivation, we should study its biogenetic roots in the elementary need for satisfaction. The deceitful motivation is an obsessing temptation, as it procures a *vain self-satisfaction* that is seductive but disastrous in its results. As long as intimate observation, indispensable as it is, does not have a methical basis, the analytical interpretation will not be scientific enough, because it is provided with a prudishly unavowed intimate observation that is made with psychological talent that is sometimes available and sometimes not. The psychological observation obtained, even if expanded by clinical observation, is too unstable to help create a solid base to support the edifice of theories.

* * *

Therefore, it is important to draw a radical line of separation. The psychology that resolves to make intimate observation—imposed by the very nature of the object of study—its principle of research is distinguished by its method from all other forms of psychology of the extraconscious. Still turning their backs to the necessity of radically revising the methods of investigation, these schools should be considered as part of classical psychology, of which they are the ultimate end, betraying the obvious methodological error one is tempted to label "physiologism."

Only after noting this essential difference is it possible to release all the admiration I feel for the great innovator of modern psychology, Freud, as well as for some of his dissident disciples, Adler and Jung. I will add a remark about Adler's work, which we will not mention again, because his considerable contribution to the problem of intrapsychic anxiety is buried under terminology that strives to deny the existence of the extraconscious functioning. His entire theoretical and therapeutic concept suffers from it, because the omnipotence he gives to the conscious and its utilitary cogitation leads him to a sort of banalization: to align to current opinions and "common sense." On the other hand, his talent for intimate observation is no less extraordinary than Freud's, and even though he is also hiding it under the pretext of proceeding exclusively through clinical observation, he succeeds in exposing the results of his exploration of the intrapsyche in a very simple manner that is freed from the Freudian apparatus of excessive systematization.

Adler discovered everyone's weaknesses in his own conscience, through the acuteness of his own intimate observation. He verified them by clinical observation that reflects them in a caricatural way. These morbid exaggerations have always existed and their intimate cause should be interpreted; Adler, inspired by Freud, discovered some of their intimate motives, such as the feeling of inferiority, the need to devaluate others in order to assure one's own superiority, and the vain tendency to place oneself at the center of attention.

Indeed, Adler found a more explanatory term, "the politics of prestige," for the manifestations of wrong motivation that Freud had somewhat hastily called "rationalizations." Consequently, Adler's influence over all contemporary psychology, although not as dramatic as Freud's, is no less profound. The uncovering of one's own intimate weaknesses exerts an effect of attraction-repulsion on everyone; one result of this effect is that, although Adler's work is rarely quoted, it is taken advantage of continuously. His discoveries were detached from his name and diffused quasi-anonymously throughout all domains of psychology. They were frequently used in the construction and interpretation of projective tests. The repercussions of Adler's discoveries extended even into Freudian schools, where—at least in nonorthodox circles—it is customary to discuss an Oedipus complex while allowing, more or less openly, a desexualized explanation of the "child-parent" relationship, as was suggested by Adler. Child psychology is currently inconceivable without the still unacknowledged use of Adler's contribution, which revolutionized the pedagogy. Although the present study of intrapsychic anxiety would have been impossible without the original orientation of Freud's teaching, it also remains indebted to Adler's discoveries. It is a great pleasure to take this opportunity to pay homage to Freud's great disciple and adversary, A. Adler.

From the interpretation of the hidden meaning of dreams, made possible by Freud's work, Jung discovered another form of extraconscious motivation: archetypes. He defines them as the residue of ethically significant collective ancestral experiences. By detecting them in dreams, Jung concluded that there existed an unconscious function that diametrically opposed the morbid subconscious that Freud discovered.

In this respect, Jung's discovery aims far. It invites psychology to study the ethical problem from an intrapsychic constellation rather than exclusively from social interactions. In fact, there is in human superconsciousness—the existence of which will be proven later—a sublimated imagination that generates ethically significant guiding images and can fight the perverse imagination which generates subconscious anxietude. Mythologies are the product of the sublime force of imagination. Jung, however, diminished the extent of his discovery by defining archetypes sometimes as mythical symbols and sometimes as the residue of ancestral experience. Myths are far from being just the product of social experience, however ancestral it may be. They are a figurative response, symbolically disguised, to an infinitely more profound and vast question concerning the existence of the universe, the genesis of life, the evolutionary destiny of the human race, the meaning of life and death of individuals, and the meaning of the life of collectivities and their cultures.

The Jungian theory attempts to complete the Freudian and Adlerian analysis by an endeavor of synthesis that is also envisioned, although differently, by existentialist philosophy. The danger of failing in the speculative interpretation is obviously as great as the project of synthesis is vast. Also, the dogmatizing ambition of classical psychology did not abdicate before the joint onslaught of the new doctrines. It found a triumphal extension in experimental psychology that rebels against the exploration of the intrapsyche and emphasizes the study of the behavior and the influence of the social environment.

An outline of all the divergent doctrines would go far beyond the framework of the present account. The fractioning of classical psychology into more contradictory tendencies indicates both the disarray that currently rules psychology and the importance of the search for an outcome. Each area of research potentially contains a valid contribution. Through the central problem of anxiety, the contributions will find the measure of their value. No other problem will tie the psychological doctrines to life. Does life not expect psychological teaching, above all else, to liberate from anxiety? This problem is significant not only for therapy; its importance extends to all manifestations of life and to all doctrines that deal with it, whether their subject is the individual more than the social environment and whether it concerns interhuman or intrapsychic relationships, behavior or intimate motives. We can emphasize that the motives—and especially their extraconscious hold—constitute the causation that essentially determines the actions, which, as a whole, form behavior (motor and organic).

*   *   *

Viewed from the perspective of the problem of anxiety and its ever-
present urgency, no task of contemporary psychology is more imperative than the discovery of whether or not extraconscious motivations
actually exist, for, if they are a psychic reality, depth psychology is far
from having extrapolated all the results from its discovery. If one were
to decide to consider these results, they would quickly put the entire
field of psychology at the intersection of all paths. The most important
of these consequences is that all the arguments against introspection
would be shown to be pretexts, the results of an extraconscious motivation, an erroneous rationalization, a prestige politics that pretends
objectivity. All of these arguments are based on the pretext that introspection could only be subjective, erroneous, and morbid. And yet, the
same introspection—even in the still unacknowledged and inadequately controlled form that it has assumed since Freud's time—eventually discovers the existence of the extraconscious motivations,
psychic phenomena that had been unknown up to now but that are ut-
terly important. Indeed, an appropriate result would be to make a systematic instrument of elucidating self-observation from this extraconscious faculty of introspection that contains an objectifying potential.

    Do we dare to foresee that this same introspection, which when
used without method, permits the discovery of wrong rationalization
(the principle of subjective blindness), once evolved into a method,
could lead to discoveries that are infinitely more significant? The rationalization directed toward motives is, in fact, a wrong motivation.
The *systematic* study of this intrapsychic process of falsification will
perhaps permit an understanding that Adler's discovery of the politics
of prestige is, in reality, a psychic phenomenon of primordial importance, a *genuine calculus* that operates unceasingly in the extraconscious and is equipped with an unsuspected precision that is subject to
certain laws. Unlike physics, where the attitude of objectivity is systematically established, psychological study encounters a blinding affectivity, a form of anxiety or false modesty, a shame that renders
objectivity unattainable for the subject unless he successfully over-
comes the shameful anxiety of becoming his own object of study.

    For psychological sciences, we all carry our own study labora-
tories within ourselves. What Freud calls "rationalization," and what
Adler named "the politics of prestige" is a wrong motivation commonly experienced, in differing degrees of intensity, by everyone. Existentialist psychology, like so many others, embroiders these discoveries by
calling them "insincerity" or "guilty conscience." Why would the psy-

chologist, among all others, be the only one who can initially confront
the intrapsychic problem in a state of clear conscience and free of all
repressing shame? This freedom, the only condition for competence,
must be acquired. How else could this occur unless one returns to
oneself? Psychology has ascertained the existence of a wrong rationalization, the politics of prestige, a dishonesty that exists in the conscience of all humans; is it conceivable that the psychologist would feel
entitled to use this discovery exclusively to observe others or to explain
the dramatic manifestations of psychopathy? It is an inhuman aberration to forget—as is, for want of time, too often the case in psychiatry—
the secret distress of the patient and to turn this oblivion into a
principle of objectivity that allows the observer to believe that he is, in
comparison to the fallen man, different in nature and higher in essence. Is it not appropriate, when confronting psychic illnesses—the
caricatural consequences of our common weaknesses—to be attentive
to this poor little interrogation that asserts itself and is truly the u-
nique condition of objectivity, the question, *What about me?*

What about me? Did I pay sufficient attention to my own tendency to rationalize my motives falsely, to be capable of glimpsing what
happens in every person's intimacy, to understand objectively the degree of bewilderment of others and have the right to judge their state
(not only from an organic point of view, but also, and primarily, from a
psychic point of view)? Only by questioning oneself in this way, and by
undertaking the authentic objectivation of oneself that it implies, can
one acquire a the right to ask a suffering individual (on condition his
or her lucidity remains intact) the salutary and therapeutic question
that is destined to awaken the feeling of responsibility: *What about
you?* Only from this essential self-interrogation can we, knowingly and
no longer extraconsciously, ask the question that generalizes the problem, and aims at the lawfulness, a goal of sciences: *What about us?* All
of us are included in the lawfulness of the psychic functioning. According to the deepest and the most shamefully hidden tendency, we all are
falsifiers of truth, with ourselves as well as with human nature in
general.

This is where the genuine psychological problem lies. Because
this problem addresses all human beings in the most direct and vexing
manner, because it touches each one's desire for prestige and touches
the common and secret politics of camouflage, it was made a taboo by
an unspoken agreement among humans. All the social conventions are
based on this agreement. Do not touch my insincerity, do not awaken
my shame and my anxiety, and I will not touch your insincerity. I would

rather undergo the actions and have you undergo my reactions; we will justify ourselves somehow or other by mutually crushing each other; at least we will both be protected from truth. But truth is not easily suppressed. It reappears from the depths of the subconscious, and that causes all individual and social miseries. The problem of anxiety is not only theoretical, it has, primarily, a practical reach: It is the problem of life. Placed at this crucial point by the discovery of the misuse of reason, or wrong rationalization, psychology that is the science of life would not fail its task, if the anxiety produced by confronting the truth did not keep it from continuing to search for the truth about anxiety.

Because of the taboo, the most redoubtable obstacle hindering this research, it would be wise to take a detour that would permit us to assemble all the elements that are likely to emphasize the biologically adaptive scope of the problem. Intimate observation, or the means of studying intrapsychic anxiety, will be eligible as a method only if its necessity and its process are proven to be the ineluctable result and even the direct extension of the evolutionary way that leads toward an ever better lucidity and foresight. With this understanding, intimate observation is the form of foreseeing lucidity, adaptively needed to overcome the intrapsychic danger, or—in other words—to control and dissolve the complications that arise from vital anxiety, which appear at the human level and are likely to assume a morbid, destructive, and involutionary character. The inadequacies of the theories of the extraconscious are not only due to the absence of a method of intimate investigation, they are also attributable to the fact that these theories are exclusively based on the study of the ontogenesis of the psychic functions. Moreover, these inadequacies are not alone. The inadequate biogenetic subfoundation leads to the confusion of the sublimation of anxiety (the incorporation in the evolutionary meaning of life) with the socialization (the adaptation to convention, imposed upon the child through parental interdictions). This psychological imprecision is due to the general situation of life sciences. The mechanistic theories of biogenesis that are currently in vogue hardly support a successful confrontation of the fundamental problem, the evolution of the human psyche.

Therefore, we need to abandon the study of intrapsychic anxiety, for the moment, in order to confront the hypothesis of a transformational dynamism of anxiety with the materialist theories of evolution. Their influence was very determining for classical psychology. It constitutes, in fact, the foundation of the whole science of life.

NOTES

1. The term *conduct*, as Janet uses it, has a double meaning. It means, on one hand, the conducting principle (motivation), and, on the other, the result of intimate elaboration (behavior). The psyche appears as the activating principle and somatic manifestations as the passive principle. Yet, the intimate motivation is not sufficiently clear. The term *action* generally refers to the motor reactions of the soma. The term *conduct* surreptitiously loses the meaning that accounts for the intimate conducting action of the psyche and now means only the manner of conducting oneself (behavior).

3

*The Foundation
of the Life Sciences*

A. MECHANISM AND FINALISM

The human psyche and its conscious and extraconscious instances is a
later product of evolution. To understand the nature of the psyche and
the laws of its functioning, it is important to know the modes of evolutionary genesis from the most primitive psychic manifestation, from
the very origin of life.

The study of the evolution of the psyche and its instances would
be significantly easier if it could be founded on the hypotheses of
genetic biology. Then we could complete these views by incorporating
the study of the psychic field as if it were an annex. This would imply
that the two branches of research (psychic functioning and psychic evolution) have a common foundation, preestablished by biology.

Unfortunately, it is essential to establish, right from the beginning, that the theoretical foundation of the current biogenetic concepts, because it is mechanistic, leaves no place for the psychic aspects
of the study of evolution. The mechanistic point of view of genetic biology strongly relates to the organicist prejudice of classical psychology
emphasized in the preceding pages: If the psyche were only a useless
ideo-affective agitation, it would not be worth paying attention to the
story of its evolution.

Research that intends to demonstrate that anxiety and its transformational dynamism is the driving force of evolution thereby introduces a hypothetical foundation irreconcilably opposed to mechanistic
transformism. This situation is unfortunate in itself and difficult for
the course of this study. To support the importance of anxiety in the

context of evolution, it will be inevitable to be critical toward spiritualism and its belief in an absolute Spirit and also toward materialism and its belief in absolute Matter. These two preestablished contradictory and irreconcilable beliefs both refer to an inexplicable absolute and use it as a principle of explanation. The absolute (ab-solute) is, by definition, lacking any solution. It has no use if one is searching for a real solution to the problems of life and existence.

Neither absolute Spirit, with its transcendental creative intentionality, nor absolute Matter, with its lack of any finalist and creative intentionality, can be the cause of the immanent intentionality, indisputably manifest in evolution, which is the essential phenomenon of life and existence.

Research that intends to demonstrate that the cause of evolution, inherent in existence, is the transformational dynamism of anxiety is forced to oppose spiritualism (for which the problem of evolution does not exist) and materialism, as well, with its various theories about evolution. All these theories are necessarily erroneous because of their common belief in absolute Matter (absolutely devoid of spirit). What a strange aberration to believe that all of life and especially its most alive aspect (so to speak)—evolution—can be reduced to an automatism.

Materialist theories and the spiritualist beliefs became so seductive in spite of their contradictions that we should be sure that the process of critique is not hindered by endless objections, drawn from an arsenal of preestablished justifications. To avoid the maze of empty discussions, let us return to the origins of the dispute and demonstrate that the premises are wrongly presented and stem from a double-faced metaphysical speculation that is superfluous and erroneous.

The exposition that will be presented may seem long and complicated at first glance. However, it does not wander away from the study of anxiety, which is the main subject here. It is indispensable as the most efficient method to eliminate the anxiety of doubt that is inseparable from wrongly established beliefs.

The problem of anxiety, which is the foundation of the dynamism of evolution, embraces all horizons of life and all questions that come to mind. The most imperative and anxiety-laden question is about life and its meaning—so long as the question remains unanswered. The word *meaning* contains a double significance: meaningful direction and value.

The scope of the problem to be solved is as follows: Are the guiding values originally transcendental and metaphysical, or are they biogenetically immanent?

B. TRANSCENDENCE AND EXISTENCE

The question of evolution naturally forces us to reexamine the origin of existence. Where does life come from? Life unfolds in time and in space; the problem expands and condenses in the question: How did the world come to exist? The most anxious interrogation inevitably follows: Why do I exist? What shall I do with my ephemeral life?

To muffle the sacred awe (anxiety), spiritualism and materialism suggest a choice of preestablished answers and, therefore, provide individuals with the option to turn their backs on the essential problem of existence and concentrate their energy on the accidental everyday problems. But the underlying contradiction about the meaning of life brings about an anxiety of disorientation that is commonly repressed and yet insidiously pervades the lives of individuals and communities.

In accordance with the transformational dynamism of anxiety, the anxiety-laden disorientation becomes an evolutionary force. It can be quieted only by elucidating the error that is the belief that the spirit, because it extends beyond the limits of time and space, discovers a time outside time and a space outside space (the metaphysical beyond), whereas, in truth, the human mind encounters only the *limit of its competence*. To identify this limit, let us call it *the mystery*, or even better, *the mysterious aspect of existence*.

We cannot overemphasize the fact that the mystery is, by definition, nonexistent. It exists only in relation to human thought. All the subsequent developments could be essentially misunderstood if we do not keep in mind the warning that *the mystery is not an entity—a thing (absolute matter)—nor is it a being (absolute spirit)*.

To understand the true significance of the term *mystery* is to cut short all metaphysical speculation. The speculation is only a futile attempt to explain the inexplicable. To establish the mysterious aspect of existence and its origin is still not sufficient. The mind in quest of certitude—precisely because it cannot grasp the mystery—should be awestruck by the unfathomable depth of existence. This awe is the religious feeling (to be distinguished from religion itself) insofar as the emotivity becomes intimate motivity: the determining cause of activities.

*   *   *

The ultimate interrogation remains, nonetheless, constraining because the emotion aroused by the mystery is a deep, sacred, and insatiable anxiety.

If reason fails to answer, another faculty of human understanding, *imagination*, will undertake to do so. The characteristic of imagination is to create suggestive images through the process of symbolic concretization and personification. *Nothing can prevent the imaginative momentum to transcend the limits of time and space, to escape into the infinite, to concretize the indefinable, but likewise nothing can put real significance into the obtained answer. The imaginative solution keeps, however, a valid significance.* The transcended images are drawn from the existing world, and their meaning, even though deprived of any real explanatory value, keeps an analogically comparative significance, which is *symbolically veracious.*

For the transcending imagination and its personifying process, the ultimate question is anthropomorphic: Who created the world and life? This formulation of the question suggests a creator to the imagination—an individual who intentionally made the world, like the human mind when it successfully fashions matter from a plan. In its attempt to compensate for the limits of reason, it costs nothing to the imagination to endow this "Creator-Being" with an absolute spirit, a creative intentionality and quasi-human feelings toward the creatures and the creation. It would be obvious, in the sequence of images, to place the Creator-Being outside the limits of time and space, in an unreal space called "Heaven" and in a time without limit called "Eternity." The entire suggestive force of these images lies in the grip they exert on emotivity (on the anxiety to be appeased); it would be incoherent to request the transcending imagination to deprive itself of its own force and to renounce the establishment of a deeply moving relationship between the Creator-Being and the "created" being. The absolute spirit, necessarily pictured as the source of all truth, inspires the failing reason of humankind and guides active orientation. It is conceived as a moral lawmaker. Thus, the fear of the impenetrable is appeased and transformed into a feeling of trust. If we follow the sequence of these emotional ties, which are introduced through images, then derangement appears as an action of punishment from the justice of the Creator-guide. The task of inspiring ethical values is added to the figurative function of creator of worlds. The transcending imagination successfully creates *a myth of profound psychological truth.* It is a psychological truth that the person who senses the unfathomable, mysterious depth of ephemeral existence through the veil of images will find in sacred anxiety the appeasement of the many forms of accidental anxietude. It is thus mythically attested that anxiety-laden restlessness, the evolutionary drive, finds its assuagement only by returning to the perfect quietude of nonexistence; nonexistence is not an absolute void and thus cannot be conceived, in the sequence of the concretizing images, as an annihilation.

The transcending imagination of myths successfully condenses the double aspect of the metaphysical mystery into a sequence of coherent images that contain a *symbolic significance*. On the one hand, it *embodies* the "beyond" of reason by the image that symbolizes it as a time-space beyond; on the other, it *personifies* the impenetrable cause of existence through the symbolic image of the "intentional Creator." By going beyond the limits of reason, the imagination assures that transcendence—a limit-idea without any real content—has an unreal content that is symbolically veracious and psychologically active because it is emotionally reassuring and incomparably beautiful. If a single myth contains symbolism of psychological reach, destined to appease sacred anxiety by extraconscious suggestion, it is, indeed, extremely likely that all myths of all peoples, despite their multiform appearances, assume, according to their secret meaning, the same psychological and vitally important function (see Diel, 1980).

As a product of the transcendental imagination, the myths are addressed only to the imagination. Their suggestive force exerts a preponderant influence on the life of communities. All cultures are based on mythologies.

The ultimate problem is not amenable to metaphysical speculation, which only succeeds in making it more inextricably complicated. It does not lend itself to a solution but to an extremely simple delimitation if it is undertaken by introspective psychology, which alone is capable of defining the limited competence of the psychic functions of reasoning and imagination. Between reasoning when it understands its limit and transcending imagination that surpasses it, there is neither contradiction nor clash.

The quarrel, and all the resulting anxiety-laden disorientation, breaks out when reasoning and imagination venture beyond their competence. An entanglement is produced that results in metaphysical speculation. *The reason starts to imagine and the imagination starts to reason.* The imaginative reasoning assumes the authority to explain transcendence. The explanation necessarily is anthropomorphic. Humans are psyche and soma, spirit and matter, and the speculative reasoning will be constrained, in its futile attempt to explain the inexplicable, to choose between a dogmatized image of the Creator-Spirit and a pseudoscientific idea of creative matter.

In spiritualism, it is necessary to make a distinction between, on one hand, the *mythically* authentic form (which could be called "imaginative hypothesis") and, on the other, the *dogmatizing* hypostasis that transforms a "hypothetical" image into a reality. A similar distinction is imperative on the subject of materialism. *The materialism of physics,* which is the basis of its exactitude, is simply a *working hypothesis.* Conversely, the *materialism of social sciences* is *metaphysical speculation,* a source of inaccuracy.

The ideological obstacle that stands against the study of intrapsychic anxiety, the essential phenomenon of life and evolution, is actually concentrated in so-called scientific exactitude. It is important to grasp this major obstacle and its raison d'être clearly.

* * *

Physics studies the motion of inanimate bodies such as, for instance, the stars. Physics did not start with the study of sidereal evolutions by chance. The regularity and vastness of this motion is so impressive that it has provided, from the earliest times, the most valuable support to spiritualistic metaphysics and its transcending finalism. The discovery of mechanical laws provided an explanation of the immanent cause and rendered the finalist explanation superfluous. This created the hope that the current star constellation as well as the history of the formation of stars could be explained in purely causal and mechanical terms, making the idea of the finalist and intentional creation appear superfluous. Astrophysics eventually conceived the *hypothesis* of a world delimited by time and space dimensions, ever filled with scattered matter that, eventually, through rotation and condensation, formed the stars and the planets.

Centuries will modify and amplify the hypothesis of astrophysics. The intention to explain (in the framework of *the hypothesis of physics*) the modalities of the formation and the motion of stars remains unchanged, *without mention of the ultimate cause of existence,* neither that of the time and space framework nor that of the matter filling it. To the question "Why does anything exist?" the physicist answers, "Framework, matter, and motion always existed." If he does not dogmatize, he will admit that this answer is not an explanation of the origins of the world, but, on the contrary, a refusal of any attempt to explain. The ultimate answer of the physicist is still hypothetical. It allows the movement, step by step, ad infinitum, away from the inevitable question of origin. We have never known of a time-space object existing forever, so it is difficult to grasp what significance such an assertion could have.

This circumspection, imposed by the limited scope of the hypothesis, is not an invitation to deny the significance of the ultimate problem. On the contrary, the hypothetical materialism of physics contains an allusion to the impenetrable principle of all existence. The hypothesis very clearly establishes the distinction between the modal and accidental causes of mechanical motion and the essential and lawful cause, called "force." *In the materialist hypothesis of physics, the notion of force remains unexplained and is regarded as inexplicable.*

To remain consistent, the physicist is constrained to note that the cause that "creates" the lawful motion of matter transcends reason. It is implicitly acknowledged that, in physics, materialism is only a working hypothesis.

Physics, brought to the limit of the inexplicable by its investigation, stops there and is content to use the symbol "force" in its abstract nudity. It declines the intervention of the imagination and its concretizing power. Suppose that physics yields to the temptation of translating its abstract symbol into a personified image—what better symbolic concretization could it find than the one proposed by mystic vision?

The transcending finalism of myths, understood as a symbol, is by no means contrary to the observation of the laws that rule the modalities of existence. The mystery of existence and the immanence of finalism are clearly manifested through these laws. The contradiction is introduced by the attempt of the social sciences to take the materialist hypothesis of physics as an absolute truth that can explain not only the origins of the Cosmos, but the origin and evolution of life as well.

*   *   *

In our culture, the discord between spiritualism and materialism has been exacerbated by the discovery of celestial mechanics. The spiritualist and materialist beliefs conflict to such an extent that the discord could well be the deepest cause of the anxious disorientation of the current period. If there were a conciliatory solution to the anxiety-laden discord, the study of anxiety should not depart from the requirement to find it and, if possible, to display it.

In fact, this solution exists. Its search left a mark on the history of Western thought from Newton to the present time. We know that to the question, "Who created celestial mechanics?" Newton wisely answered: "the Clock-Maker, the demiurge." His answer undoubtedly was meant to express his belief in a mystery that overreaches the competence of astrophysics, and it leads us to think that Newton was not fooled by *perceptive empirism, for which the solar systems and galaxies—confined in the fixed frame of time and space—have always existed.*

Nevertheless, the *materialist theories of evolution*—while they are based on celestial mechanics—have the tendency to forget the "Clock-Maker." Nothing would be more instructive than to dwell upon the extent of this omission.

Astrophysics is entitled to develop its hypothesis with the imperative provision that it does not forget that it proposes a fiction, according to which *everything happened in accordance with its hypothetical reconstruction, as if humans had witnessed the scene;* because the spatial scene is created wherever the eye is open and does not exist without the eye's presence. If we conceive of a time preceding life, when the gestation of the spatial universe has been accomplished, we are transporting ourselves in imagination, without taking notice of it, to an era that has long since vanished and into sidereal space. Thus, paradoxically, we believe we are witnessing a scene that supposedly has happened when no life was present. Simply eliminate yourself as a spectator to feel the illusion fall apart. Now that the supposed spectator has disappeared, and the matter supposed to be in gestation not being able to perceive itself, what determinable meaning could we grant an existence that does not exist, either for itself or for others, for it is neither perceived nor emotionally experienced. Is not this nonexisting existence also appropriate for the earth that supposedly existed before the advent of life? With this collapse, the illusion of perceptive empiricism gives way to a vertigo of fear that is actually the sacred anxiety of mystery.

The truth of astrophysics is not absolute; it is relative to the anthropos. It remains mathematically true that, in effect, everything would have happened in the way the anthropos is reconstituting it, if he had lived in the gestative universe that, by way of evolution, became the universe in which humans see themselves and currently feel themselves to be alive; a universe that is for them their full reality, but that exists only relative to their perceptions.

This relativity, although veracious and real, is valid for all sciences that have the common and restricted aim of studying perceived phenomena. Among others, this is true for geology, with its study of the stratigraphic stages and the fossils they enclose, a testimony to the successive appearances of life forms that are more and more highly organized. Skeletal reconstruction successfully represents the animal in accordance with the perception of humans—if they had lived in those earliest times.

Differing from all other sciences, *the study of evolution* infallibly leads to the question without answer: Where does the existence of scattered matter in space come from? And, especially, where does the immanent organizing spirit and its law of harmony (ever perturbed and reconstituted) come from?

Even the galaxies, apparently immutable throughout time, are subject to the law or the spirit that presides *over temporal unfolding* and requires, rather than a fixed and stable harmony, a ceaseless evolutionary reharmonization that is the primordial condition of existence (including the destruction of life: death). The deepest transformational dynamism of anxiety comes from this.

*   *   *

Finally, humans, through their interest in the problem of evolution, intend to know, rather than the evolutionary history of the matter-soma, the biogenetic history of the organizing spirit that, in humans, becomes conscious spirit. The burst of consciousness made human beings thinking animals, beings that individually and collectively must search for their own harmonizing path (the harmony of desires), their own way of evolutionary improvement; otherwise they fall into the anxiety of disorientation. Human beings won't find their own way without the search for essential harmony: the harmony of thought that encompasses all the data of existence (psyche, soma, and environment) but excludes the fruitless attempt to explain the mystery.

The study of the evolutionary stages that lead from preconscious mind to the opening of the human mind, which is half-conscious and half-affectively blind, is the genuine problem of evolution. This stage that modern humankind has attained is destined to evolve toward an ever more lucid and clairvoyant state.

While this essential aspect is forgotten, the materialist evolutionism is building upon the attempt to use the hypothesis of astrophysics and its method of mechanistic explanation to study vital phenomena. Moreover, one can comprehend the whole extent of the temptation. After all, it seems natural to hope that the increase of mechanistic development will be able to ward off transcending finalist dogma, in relation not only to the creation of the stars and our planet, but also the creation of life.

This is the formulation of the development upon which the life sciences are based: On our planet, life eventually appeared. Life is not exclusively created by the mechanicist movement that condenses matter into heavenly bodies, but it allegedly originates from that same inert matter owing to a molecular motion that is mechano-chemical in character. The evolutionary transformations are also the effect of a cellular chemism, allegedly capable of gradually sensitizing matter. Therefore the psychic sensibilization is supposedly just an epiphenomenon. Considering the extreme economy of this hypothesis, it may seem unimportant that experience doesn't successfully illustrate it. Maybe someday it will. If not, are we not entitled to assert that laboratory experience will undoubtedly be incapable of reconstituting the infinitely vaster conditions realized in nature? We certainly are entitled to promote such arguments. Because of the lack of verifications it remains, nonetheless, that these are merely eventualities; that should prompt a certain caution regarding the expansion of the materialist hypothesis. The stakes are too great to justify the attempt to elevate this hypothesis to the dogma that is the unquestioned foundation of the life sciences, for the sole concern of economy.

Caution is advised all the more because the economy is doubtful. To hope that one can arrive at a unified concept that encompasses all the phenomena of life and nature by expanding the founding principles of physics could be justifiable *providing one ensures that the proposed prolongation takes into account all the guiding principles of physics*, including not only the materialist hypothesis, but also the hypothesis of force. This indispensable condition is not met. To expose this serious gap should be sufficient for the materialist hypothesis of the origin and evolution of life to lose its credibility.

*   *   *

For it is an insolvable contradiction, not a reparable omission. To include in the study of vital phenomena the equivalent of force in physics necessarily requires the introduction of the term *vital force*. In conformity with the significance of the term *force in physics*, the term *vital force* should contain only the necessary observation of the mysterious aspect that underlies all phenomena of existence, including all phenomena of life. The dispute between vitalism and mechanism in the life sciences rests on an error that a physicist would not make regarding the term *force*. The vitalists are correct to introduce the term *vital force*, but wrong to view it as a means of explanation; mechanicists can reject the vitalist explanation as occult, but they shouldn't oppose the introduction of this term. To the lawfulness of mechanism in physics, which is inexplicable as to its cause, corresponds the distinctive trait "animation" for living matter, no less inexplicable for the life sciences. If animation is inexplicable, the wish to explain it as the result of a simple mechano-chemical arrangement is futile. To explain satisfactorily the origin of life from inert matter is not possible. Matter is either completely inert and no process can generate life from it, or it is not totally inert and its evolution toward manifestly animated forms is not exclusively due to the mechano-chemical process. The evolutionary continuity between life and inertia is impossible to establish.

The omission of "force" is contrary to the guiding principles of physics; it destroys the economic continuity, the only raison d'être of the mechanicist hypothesis in social sciences. If the hypothetical prolongation has no reason to be, we can as well say that it is contrary to reason.

The prolongation that intends to introduce mechanicity into the study of life is contrary to reason, for it is merely an imaginative speculation disguised as reasoning. By attempting to exclude the notion of the mysterious force—in which is concentrated, in physics, the ultimate question that must be left unanswered—the life sciences conclude that nothing is inexplicable. The intention of the doctrine is not only to reduce the evolutionary modes to a mechanism, but to explain the origin of life and even its mysterious principle. Concrete matter, the object of physical study, becomes an abstract and absolute principle that is supposedly inaccessible to any critical attempts. Materialism, a simple hypothesis in physics, acquires the character of a metaphysical dogma in the life sciences.

* * *

There is a difference between the foundation of the life sciences and the foundation of physics. Physics elaborated its basic principle independently of any interference or imitation, exclusively from the demands dictated by its own research. The instability of the foundation of the social sciences is due to the fact that they evaded the obligation to lay their foundation authentically and autonomously. Responsible for *animated matter* rather than supposedly inert matter, and somewhat at a loss because of the difficulty of the task, it is not surprising that the life sciences attempt to rely on the standard science called physics.

C. RESEARCH OF A METHODICAL FOUNDATION OF THOUGHT

In all the great cultures of the past, an epoch of philosophical thought existed between theological spiritualism and antitheological materialism. To remain sincere in its effort of penetration, philosophical speculation, originally metaphysics, became self-criticism of the mind, which aspires to the elaboration of a "theory of knowledge."

In Western culture, the "Cartesian cogito" introduced the decisive penetration:

Doubt is anxiety of the mind in quest of truth.

The Cartesian doubt opens a new era in Western thought. It is an important point to understand how and why the anxiety-laden chaos of the current ideologies is related to the fact that the research, triggered by Cartesian doubt, is incomplete.

In the final analysis, the sudden appearance of the evolutionist concept professed by Lamarck is responsible for this incomplete state of affairs. The evolutionist concept triggered a swarm of ideas and theories that captivated the attention and distracted it from the elaboration of a theory of knowledge. This theory should precede all research that aims at returning to the origins of existence, the world, and life, as does evolutionism.

The materialist theories of evolution, proud of their cogito influence, could have gained a greater advantage by taking into account the developments of the Cartesian formula that—we will refer to them later—were, in fact, the first to suggest the idea of evolution (Fichte, Schelling, Hegel).

Materialist transformism, by knowing this essential fact, could have avoided the no less essential error to base its theories on *perceptive empiricism*, which was long fought by the theory of knowledge, the greatest merit of which was to develop *perceptive idealism*, entirely verified today by nuclear physics.

Perceptive empiricism is not a theory. It is established on the apparently obvious fact that persuades us that the world exists as our organs of perception present it to us. Perceptive idealism, which is the theory expressed by philosophical criticism, is based on the rather obvious fact that the perceived world depends on the specificity of the perceptive organs.

The opposition between perceptive and reflexive evidence forces us to admit that one of them is only pseudoevidence. Nuclear physics, which is a decisive penetration of Newtonian physics (based on perceptive empiricism), settles the dilemma in favor of *idealism*, by proving the relativity of time which includes the relativity of time, space. If the time and space frame is not of an absolute origin, once and for all preestablished, the matter that fills it does not exist in an absolute way, either.

Physics uses its formulas of time, space, and matter relativity exclusively in the restricted domain of nuclear research. It has no need to expand it into a theory of knowledge; its problem is not to know the origin of matter, but to study exclusively the laws that rule the motion of matter, permitting even nuclear physics to be content with a working hypothesis based on perceptive empiricism.

*   *   *

The greatest problem posed by the theory of knowledge can be accessed by a process diametrically opposed to the philosophical process. It is preferable to use the critique of perceptive empiricism as a starting point rather than, like philosophy, ending up with it. This allows us to make a more lively and explicit presentation of the indispensable penetration that usually seems harsh and difficult:

> *Psychic functions operate only with the support of*
> *somatic organs, such as perceptive organs.*

The perception of spatial range is common to every being endowed with distance vision. What idea can we have, though, of the olfactory universe of beings as close to us as mammals? What environment does the insect delineate with its faceted eyes and antennas? If only insects were existing, would it be reasonable to pretend that the universe as perceived by humans actually existed? Nevertheless, it would be one of the infinite number of universes virtually preexisting "within the mystery."

The mystery is nothing but this always preexisting virtuality that comprises an infinite number of universes that never were and, perhaps or undoubtedly, never will be perceptively realized. From this infinite virtuality emerges an infinite number of galaxies, populated by an infinite number of unimaginable organisms, equipped with no less unimaginable perceptive organs.

To our tactile and visual organs, the perceived objects have a material density, a spatial form, and a temporal duration. The material substance and temporal subsistence, however, are but qualities we have attributed to objects by our way to perceive. Doesn't physics teach us that, in actuality, these phenomena can be reduced to the mysterious force of attraction and repulsion? The mass is susceptible to transformation into an energy that is no longer visually perceptible, or perceptible by touch.

As dense as they appear to us, objects can be penetrated without resistance by certain radiations (X and gamma, for example) for which they become quasi-nonexistent. Why would it be impossible that some organisms that live on our planet or elsewhere could be equipped with organs able to pierce through matter and render it nonexistent to them, or rather existent in the form of energetic centers? Indeed, matter offers a weak resistance to acoustic waves, even for the human ear.

It would be a foolish anthropomorphism to believe that humankind alone is the measure of all that exists, and that the infinite mystery is the most explicitly and perfectly manifested in the universe perceived by humans. All universes, even though differently perceived, share the law that rules their perceptive appearance. The mathematical formula grasps this mysterious lawfulness, which is immanent to all forms of existence and provides a perfect reflection of it.

It is, also, the conclusion derived by nuclear physics. The atom is pure law, pure materialized spirit. The spatialized image that is the nucleus with its satellites—the electrons—is only a schematic representation. What is true for one atom is also true for the entirety of atoms: the perceived universe.

The inevitable necessity that dictates the mutual unfolding of the bipolarized modes (spirit / matter, or equivalently, psyche / world) "precedes" the living world, that is, the experienced universes.

The evolutionary unfolding is accomplished by the lawfulness that analogically prefigures, in the universes perceived by animals, the universe that humans will perceive when, in the course of evolution, they appear in it.

This adjustment of perceptive empiricism brings a simple solution to a problem that is subsequent to epistemology: How is it possible for the spirit to know the world veraciously? It knows it through preadaptation. The objectal[1] world that is perceived by humans is *objectively* reflected in their thought, because it is the lawfully complementary object of the thinking subject. *The causal thought of the now-conscious being is apt to represent the world* (which has eventually expanded into a multitude of objects) veraciously, *because the thinking subject and the objectal world are evolved modalities of the lawful bipolarity that characterized existence from the very beginning.*

This methodological observation considers only the modal relations of existence. However, it leads to a simplified formulation of the relation between the modal and the mysterious aspect: *Psyche and world are the true appearance of the inexplicable.* This formula conveys the equivalence of the two modes; it emphasizes that their "cause" is not explainable by reasoning but, rather, transcends reason.

The formula opposes materialism that declares the psyche is an epiphenomenal manifestation of the soma, as well as certain spiritualist doctrines for which the world is an illusory manifestation of the psyche. The two modes of existence are not an appearance, but a reality perceptively and emotively experienced. There is no matter without spirit, nor spirit without matter. The world starts with life; life starts with the world.

Life and the world are united in mystery. The mystery is not an entity outside the world. The world possesses an immanently mysterious aspect manifested through the organizing and evolutionary interinfluence that exists between spirit and matter.

The spirit is not the exclusive property of humankind; the preconscious spirit was originally the organizer of matter and it became, through evolution, the animator of the soma-matter: the organizer of the perceptive organs that are an earlier stage of the psychic manifestation—the instinctive foresight of higher animals. Preconscious spirit eventually becomes half-conscious in humans. Evolutionary finalism, which tends toward ever increased lucidity (the best means of adaptation), will undoubtedly surpass the present degree of clear-sightedness. At the current degree of its evolution, the spirit is, on one hand, introspective, valuating the desires that bind humans to the objectal environment, and, on the other, it also explains the environmental world.

The immanent meaning, the immanent finalism of life in evolution, is *the progressive spiritualization of matter and the progressive materialization of the spirit.* "The incarnation of the spirit" is the profound meaning that underlies the mythology of all peoples and is the foundation of their cultures. Through the symbol "incarnation," the mythical prescience foreshadows the biological immanence of the meaning and value of life. At the human level, the evolutionary meaning becomes *the immanent imperative ethics that is biologically grounded.*

D. FROM THE COGITO TO INTROSPECTIVE PSYCHOLOGY

The return to origins eliminates the absolute as a principle of explanation and *legitimizes the exposition of immanent finalism* (subsequently to be completed). It is important to extract the *methodological conclusions* that will dominate the study of *the evolution of the psyche* in the second part of this work.

Let us stop for a moment to orient ourselves in relation to the historical situation that results from the meeting, interinfluence, and contradiction of various trends of thought.

The most essential and profound cause of the present chaos of beliefs and ideologies is the fact that the philosophical rough draft of a methodology of thought is still incomplete. Because of this situation, it is good to summarize, even if very briefly, the masterly effort of methodological penetration that Descartes started with the *Discourse on Method* and that Hegel pursued with *The Phenomenology of Mind*.

The Cartesian doubt aimed to challenge the speculative formulation of the ultimate question as posed by scholastic philosophy, "Who created the world" (confined in the time/space frame)? This formulation of the question of origins leaves no possibility for doubt about an intentional creation. According to scholastics, the creator who is placed outside the temporal/spatial existence and outside doubt is the ultimate certainty. It has been demonstrated that this position contains a misinterpretation; the question is posed in an imaginative form and the answer is taken as a logical and explanatory affirmation.

Descartes, seeking a basic certainty protected from doubt as well as from belief, suggested as a starting point the statement of subjective evidence: "I am." Then, he was led to ask: "How is it that I am?" Rather than transcend the answer and look for the inaccessible "cause" (by making a concept out of the symbol "Creator"), Descartes was content to envision the *mode* from which the certainty of existing proceeds: "I am because my thought cannot question my existence." I think *myself*, therefore I am. His answer affirms that psychic life, or animated matter, does not exist because it originates from inert matter, but exists because life and the world *are reflected in this more evolved modality that is the human mind* and have thus become objects of contemplation.

Cartesian doubt opposed intentional transcendence. But Descartes's critical thought already attacks, although implicitly, *the condition inseparable from an intentional creation: the notion of a time / space framework*, which is the boundary between the creator and the created world. However, the Cartesian formula suggests the belief in another fixed frame; that of the human mind, fancied *exclusively conscious* and the only criterion of existence. Since lower beings do not think, they therefore do not exist or have any life; they would then be only automatons. The evolutionary continuity is radically brought to a halt.

Thus, Descartes deprives himself of the possibility, or of the

necessity, to introduce the immanent intentionality of nature manifested through evolutionary finalism in place of transcendental intentionality. The stratified world—all objects, including the automaton-
animal—would be an illusion of the subject. Conversely, the absence of
finalism, whether transcendental or immanent, was the error that contained the invitation to the materialist interpretation. Descartes found
himself with the impossibility of establishing a bridge between the
subject's thought and the world of objects; despite his original intention, he was constrained to reintroduce the transcendental finalism.
From the statement "I think, therefore I am," he concluded: "I am,
therefore God is." All the work of elucidation prompted by the valid intention of the Cartesian formula is therefore to be started again.

The movement of revision began with the *Solipsism of Berkeley*,
which developed Cartesian subjectivism to its end result. If nothing exists other than the thinking subject, is it certain that other people
think and exist? Perceived as inhabitants of the world-appearance,
wouldn't they be also simple appearances produced by the only subject
that can be proven to think—the ego that alone would exist to the exclusion of the real existence of others?

Locke seeks the solution to this dead end. By diverting the attention away from the me-subject toward the *perceived world, he justly
demonstrates that for all persons most qualities (color, flavor, density,
and the like) of objects are but appearances conditioned by sensory perception.* Objects do not exist in themselves such as they appear to us;
this applies also to the object-other as a body and even for the body of
the person that perceives. As Berkeley put it, others do not exist such
as they are perceived; not only that, the person as a body is only an appearance and this is what allows Locke to save—against Berkeley—
the existence of others as psyches. All individuals as psyches can create
a perceived world that is common to all. (If Locke did not explicitly
draw this conclusion, it should be considered, nevertheless, as the implicit intention of his thought.) This conception does not sufficiently
correct the Cartesian proposition. It considers only the individual who
perceives and does not guarantee the objectivity of the individual's
thought.

This is why Hume is opposed to this tentative rectification. If the
objectal world were an appearance of the psyche, why wouldn't the
links of causality, which are established by the individual's thought,
also be an appearance falsely considered a chain of cause and effect?
Thus, doubt turns against the only evidence admitted by Descartes. It
is fastened to thought, supreme quality of the individual. The Car-

tesian doubt is transformed into a generalized skepticism.

Kant attempts to overcome skepticism. In Kant's theory, the world is still viewed as an appearance of the psyche; however, it is not a semblance, but a *phenomenal reality* (consensus data) because everyone's psyche is endowed with the same manner of perceiving and thinking that, ineluctably and a priori, precedes any actual act of perception or reflection. Each object is perceived as a substance endowed with modifiable attributes (big or small, hot or cold, solid or liquid) and, for our mind, the modifications of the attributes inevitably operate as a chain of cause and effect. These a priori forms, these cognitive and perceptive "molds," require the inception of a *mysteriously preexisting* "in-itself," from which human beings (themselves somatic substances, subject to causal modifications) delineate the environment they perceive. No perceptive or cognitive act being possible outside these preexisting "molds," causality is not a subjective habit that could tolerate an exception, as claims Hume, but it is the immutable law that governs all existence; this ensures the perceptive world, with its characteristics of objectal appearance, and thought, with its objective veraciousness. This conception is, however, too static. The molds of perception and cognition are considered a priori forms exclusively proper to humankind. The animal (the animated being) is again seen as an automaton. Thus Kant—like Descartes—is tempted to reintroduce the transcending intentionality. Believing ethics unthinkable without the existence of an absolute spirit that infuses it, Kant eventually turns his mysterious "in-itself" into a spirit-lawmaker dictating the ethical values to humankind. This is a correct mythical image, but is an erroneous "postulate of reason."

Fichte, Schelling, Hegel, all Kant's successors, oppose this overly static and metaphysical—in the doctrinal sense—concept. They introduce the *idea of evolution* that is accomplished by a dialectic movement that oscillates between the ego and the nonego (the subject and the object). The subject exists only by distinguishing itself from the object; and at each step of the evolutionary enlightenment of this distinction corresponds a more conscious subject, that can, out of the in-itself, cut out a time/space world more clearly differentiated in a variety of objects. The metaphysical speculation is not yet eliminated. Hegel's new spiritualism puts forth the supreme quality of the psyche (the latest product of evolution)—the mind—as an absolute principle. Evolution is defined as the successive inceptions of the transcending mind. The mystery, again, is anthropomorphized.

Hegel's *The Phenomenology of Mind* (1831), particularly, exerted

a persisting influence that is still perceptible today. Existentialism and
phenomenology still take the conscious subject as foundation for existence. They intend to extract existence from the thinking subject,
thanks to the play of dialectics that is more or less related to Hegel's
method of thesis-antithesis and is distantly inspired by the Cartesian
proposition of the omnipotence of conscious thought.

*   *   *

Today, materialism and neospiritualism confront each other in the
realm of science and, particularly, in the life sciences. Neospiritualism
is faithful to perceptive idealism, and materialism returns to perceptive empiricism. This underlying contradiction, which is secretly hidden in the foundations of doctrines, causes a confusion, the misdeeds
of which spread from the theoretical to the practical domain.

The sole trait common to neospiritualism and materialism is that
they both refer to the Cartesian cogito and, above all, to Hegel's dialectics. The neo-spiritualist doctrines of existentialism and phenomenology have, in some way, rallied materialism in the common aim to
fight the transcendental finalism of the various theologies.

Existentialism and phenomenology, concerned only with explaining existing phenomena, though far from accepting materialist mechanisms, both view in transcendence not relative (in relation to reason)
but absolute nonexistence, nothingness. By reintroducing the absolute
and making nothingness out of the mystery, do they not deny the
mystery and turn phenomenal existence into a principle that is too absolute and existential anxiety into an insurmountable phenomenon?
Thus, we encounter under the heading of "existentialism" some doctrines that attempt to avoid this incoherence by reintroducing the absolute spirit. (It is essential to add that these few succinct remarks are
designed to give a general outline; they are far from rendering justice
to a movement of ideas that, historically speaking, should be considered a link in the effort of elucidation, common to all directions of research—even if divergent).

The diversity of theoretical solutions finally reaches the domain
of social life. The theoretical discord becomes known and expands into
two main streams. The first is due exclusively to metaphysical anxiety
and rebels against any attack regardless of where it originates. Theologies still seek solace in the old beliefs issued from the dogmatization
of the transcending symbolism of myths. One intention of religions is
to ensure that values remain absolute; they see in values the only possible fortification against the cynical triumph of amoralism. The other

stream, of no less considerable significance, arises from the growing anxiety of everyday life routine disorientation; the ensuing confusion shakes the foundations of social life. The move to reoganize social life and its material needs retains the method of development by thesis and antithesis from Hegel's spiritualist phenomenology. By developing dialectics into an instrument for analyzing the economic structure of societies, dialectical materialism joins the ranks of materialist positivism, the current foundation of the life sciences.

* * *

The anxiety-laden disorientation of our time occurs as a consequence of all those contradictory ideologies. A thorough analysis of anxiety is impossible without first exposing its most fundamental cause: the vertigo produced by facing the unfathomable depths of life that provoke the bewilderment of reason and the exceeding of the measure of its rights and limits. No longer under the control of reason, the imagination is exalted and wanders into obsessive speculations and incoherent actions. The bewilderment of reason and its corresponding imaginative exaltation are the most profound causes of mental insanity and of its consequent affective and active disorientation.

There are metaphysical beliefs in all ages. However, when beliefs become contradictory, the disorientation threatens to acquire a pathological aspect. The disputes soon shake the value judgments that guide activities. The anxiety-laden contradiction does not exist only in the conscience of individuals. Within society, groups are forming with beliefs or ideas that, when they clash, either disintegrate or mutually fantasize each other. All life risks degenerate into traumatic situations, which is likely to make the individual's anxiety-laden disorientation even more morbid. The uneasiness of the spirit that characterizes the epoch in general eventually produced a swarm of mental illnesses, ranging from nervous irritability to loss of reason.

From that point of view, the appearance of *depth psychology* and its search for a curative method is due to the ineluctable need to complete, by more appropriate means, the self-criticism of thought that Descartes inaugurated. Depth psychology inherits this essential problem all the more because metaphysical anxiety and its temptation to create ineffective solaces are a sign of the motivation hidden in the depths of the extraconscious. In order to be truly efficient, the therapy needs to be based on the comprehension of the extraconscious symbolic productions called *psychopathological symptoms, dreams, and myths*, to the exclusion of all metaphysical speculation.

Study of the extraconscious and its symbolic expressions (super-conscious mythologies and subconscious symptoms) inevitably leads psychology back to the essential problem of meaningful or meaningless (sound or pathological) conduct and, therefore, back to the ultimate question of the immanent or transcending origin of values.

Epistemological philosophy could not complete its methodologi-cal quest because it was based exclusively upon conscious thought. The psychology of intimate motivations is compelled to analyze the secret motives of persisting metaphysical speculation, which encourages one to accept conventional solutions. These subconscious motives are nu-merous and complex. But, it is also true that an epistemologically profound doubt persists, in varying degrees of intensity, in each person's ethical superconsciousness: the call of the spirit, the aspira-tion to truth.

The conflict between subconscious temptation and supercon-scious aspiration is the central phenomenon of each individual's life, the cause of profound anxiety (too often dispersed in a multitude of ac-cidental anxieties). The central conflict—while immanent for every-one—generally escapes conscious detection. It is buried in the depths of the extraconscious, where the repressing subconscious often prevails over superconscious prescience (manifest in dream symbology). The es-sential assuagement will be found by a psychological science, methodi-cally established by liberating and elucidating introspection.

* * *

The necessary recourse to introspection is already implicitly contained in the Cartesian cogito: If *thought* is the measure of existence, the en-tire *epistemological problem becomes a psychological problem*, for thought is a psychic function.

Thought, insofar as it remains lucid and despite subconscious blinding, should introspectively self-control to liberate itself from the obsessive motives of arrogance and its vain pretense to explain the mystery of existence. The complementary methodological principle fol-lows: *The thought liberated from the futile metaphysical quarrel should concentrate on the study of these two modalities of existence—psyche and world—and their evolutionary and involutionary modifications.*

E. METHODOLOGICAL CONCLUSIONS

In the previous analyses we extracted the principles that will sub-sequently guide the detailed study of the transformational dynamism of anxiety. The essential point is to understand that evolution is an infinitely more vast and more profound phenomenon than materialistic evolutionalism has suggested.

The transformational dynamism of anxiety, a somatopsychic phenomenon, relates not only to the evolution of the soma but also to that of the psyche. The psychosomatic organism, in the course of its evolution, acquires increasingly more evolved perceptive organs and psychic perceptibility, which then conditions a more distinctly perceived objectal environment. *Psyche, soma, and environment concomitantly evolve.*

The anthropos is the only being that thinks about evolution. *His primary interest is his own evolutionary origin.* He builds explanatory theories about his origin and his evolutionary past. However, no logical link exists between species. The lower species is not the cause of the appearance of the higher species and the higher species is not the effect of the lower species. *The link between species is not logical; it is analogical.*

Since each evolutionary step is an advance toward the anthropos, the somatic analogies are clearly manifest (in higher multicellular life forms) in the position of the limbs and of the internal organs, and especially in the progressive cerebration of the nervous system, the somatic support of psychic life. The first indication of a nervous system is already observable in some unicellular creatures. *Somatic* evolution and its study progress upward from the unicellular to the anthropos.

On the contrary, the analogies that link together the stages of the evolution of intimate *psychic* functioning are inaccessible to direct observation. These analogies can be revealed only by a thinking being's self-observation. In this case, the analogical explanation has to *descend* from the study of the most highly evolved psychic organization, which is directly experienced by humans, to the rudimentary organization of the psychic life of the most primitive beings. This analogical method subsequently will be studied in detail.

It is essential to recall that the analogical explanation from the monad to human does not concern the mysterious aspect of evolution (the universes specified by each being's perception of them) but its unavoidable anthropomorphized aspect. The anthropos can perceive and study the evolutionary lineage, in which he is a link, only at the level of his own vital space (as he is, in turn, included in other species' vital space but in a form analogically tied to their own self-perception).

In the theory of evolution, the analogical conclusion is the best method, because nature itself proceeds by way of analogical unfolding, evolutionary step by evolutionary step. However, the analogical meth-

od—no less than intimate observation—comes up against the principle
of suspicion. It is, therefore, necessary to insist upon the conditions of
its legitimate use.

*   *   *

Every method has its sources of error, objectal observation no less than
intimate observation, and logical conclusion no less than analogical
conclusion. Analogy is considered inferior to logical thought because,
as a still undisciplined form, it generated the human species' effort of
orientation (animism) and also because the analogical vision was used
rather arbitrarily during the whole cultural history. Logical thought
and its methods of experimental observation, on the other hand, are a
later product of the faculty of reason; therefore, they seem to be more
evolved. However, analogical thought, since the very beginning and in
its animist form, made every effort to unveil the meaning of existence,
thereby accomplishing the principal function of comprehension. The
inadequacy of this primitive effort does not reside in its analogical process but in the fact that, by failing to recognize the nature of the phenomena to be explained, the analogies were imprecise and often purely
formal. The quest for the essential throughout the multitude of apparent forms had a divinatory and metaphorical character. (Poetry, by
its metaphorical language, offers a proof of the elementary force that
is inherent to analogical intuition.) In the realm of science, however,
this inexhaustible force cannot become fertile without being submitted
to a discipline; this would permit the bypass of the purely *formal*
analogies, which, disturbing the coherence of *lawful* analogies, confer
a speculative character to thought. That is where the critical intellect
should intervene. A later form of comprehension because it is less essential than analogy and in fact more a complementary tool, the logical intellect has the task of submitting, to the synthesis of the mind, a
multitude of details judiciously observed and logically clarified.

   The analogical mind and the logical intellect should complement
each other. The spirit seeks a comprehensive vision in which the
details, provided by the intellect, are classified, harmonized, and crys-
tallized. Because of the synthesizing power of analogical thought, the
spirit becomes creator of truth. The analogical conclusions contain the
creative principle because they engender one another. They acclaim,
support, and mutually complete each other. *No truth should or could
contradict another truth.* Each truth should be incorporated into the
whole, in order for the anxiety of doubt to be quieted and for the joy of
knowledge to manifest in its place.

The most significant conquests of science rest upon analogical conclusions. It is said that a falling apple revealed, for Newton, the laws of astral motion. No logical conclusion could succeed in putting the two phenomena together. Intuitively guided by analogical thought, Newton ventured to conclude that a mysterious force existed that, in physics, is the attraction of masses. (The apple is attracted by the earth as the earth is attracted by the sun.) This is the masterful analogical intuition that pioneered the discovery of the laws of mechanics. The analogical expansion led to the elaboration of physics. After Michelson's experiment, the result of which threatened to ruin the lawful harmony of Newtonian physics, Einstein proved that coherence could be reestablished provided that one comprehends Newtonian physics as a special case analogically tied to a vaster harmonious ensemble.

* * *

In the domain of social sciences, the two forms of comprehension, logical and analogical, came to dissociate and even disagree rather than complement each other. Behaviorism, currently in vogue, undertakes to explain the evolutionary relationship between animals and humans by the exclusive use of logical thought. In order to attain its aim, it accumulates experiment upon experiment, which happen to be very instructive, about the somatic reactions of animals. Behaviorism, for fear of being compelled, by the use of analogical comparison, toward conclusions that would grant anthropomorphic feelings to the animal, lays its foundation upon the supposition that the animal is an automaton, deprived of any feeling life. The supposition is brought to the level of a pretended certitude by a basic formula stipulating that an animal's actions, its behavior, are *automatic responses* to environmental stimulation. What should be proven (the absence of psychic life between stimulus and response) is asserted as a postulate under the pretext of experimental objectivity.

For the sake of the materialist cause, behaviorism suggests something most unlikely. It forgets that the animal is an animated being. Unable to deny the existence of the material and sexual organic needs in animals, it finally mentions a need for satisfaction, forgetting that satisfaction and dissatisfaction are feelings that prove the existence of a psychic functioning inserted between stimulus and response even in the most primitive being. The false—because purely formal—analogy of behaviorism that compares the animal to an inanimate automaton should, therefore, be replaced with the search for analogies that tie the somatopsychic life of animals to the psychosomatic life of humans.

Analogy is not an identity. In order not to be formal, the analogy should be based on the *definition of the common traits and differential traits*. Obviously, it would be erroneous to grant animals the nuanced wealth of human feelings. (The animal is animated with emotion. Its nutritional and sexual appetites are rooted in the elementary need for self-preservation and preservation of the species.) In humans, the elementary emotivity, which awakens when faced with the problem of life and death, is dispersed in innumerable emotional agitations and in multiple desires, each of which could become a motive for future action. The life of feelings is both enriched and impoverished. Rarely are humans deeply moved, in the fullest sense of the word. They are superficially affected, and this affectivity easily degrades into affectation. However, the analogy remains and covers the range from the life of feelings to the active search for satisfactions. The latter is provided, in higher animals, by the foreseeing instinct and in humans by foreseeing thought. Foresight is the common trait; the degree of lucidity provides the differential trait.

Behaviorist experiments are rich in lessons about animal life, as the instinctivity and the feelings that determine the response to a given stimulus do not vary for animals of the same species. The response obtained by the experimental stimulation of a single animal is valid for the behavior of the species. As the psychic functioning is not individual, the laboratory experiment can discard it, provided it doesn't view it as nonexistent or as a negligible epiphenomenon. If the psychic functioning, invariable in any given species that has been experimented with, is negligible for the experimenter, it is, however, not negligible for the life of the anima, which, as a whole, is the phenomenon to be studied.

The behaviorist method, thus established, can be applied to every animal species. This is only one step removed from believing oneself in authority to include the thinking species not, of course, by experimentation, but by a false analogical conclusion. Behaviorism does not hesitate to take this false step.

By refusing to use the analogical comparison to draw conclusions from humans to animals, behaviorism is finally misusing analogical thought by pseudologically concluding, from the pretended absence of psychic life in animals, that there is absence of an authentic psychic life in humans.

The entire intimate life of human beings, all the intimate deliberation that is inexhaustibly in operation to elaborate a willed decision, is pretended nonexistent and vitally superfluous. What does it matter whether or not it inserts itself between stimulus and response, since it is only a negligible epiphenomenon? Because, if behaviorism acknowledged deliberation, it should admit, as well, that psychic functioning assumes a vitally important purpose. At least, it ought to be studied. By which method, however?

Behaviorism's error is not only inauspicious to the comprehension of the evolutionary problem; it extends to all domains of social sciences. The psychology of human behavior bases itself on behaviorism and pretends that its task consists exclusively of the study of human behavior, of human conduct.

In turn, sociology, which is based on the formula "stimulus-response," pretends that the character of individuals, deprived of any autonomy, is wholly a product of social environment, that the guiding values are the product of social conventions, that a society is more than the sum total of its individuals, and so on. All these propositions, which reduce the individual to an automaton, are a consequence of the insufficient distinction between *motives* and *goals* of actions. Goals are accidental determining factors. They mobilize intrapsychic energy, which is an inner tension, or the intentions that, in everyone, are preelaborated in the form of intimate motives, the essential determining factors of future reactions and, therefore, of social interreactions.

* * *

The central problem of evolution, which is the subject of the second part of the present work, is the biogenesis of the psyche. Before approaching the study of psychic evolution, it is essential to define clearly what definition of the term *psyche* will be used. We wish to establish, as clearly as possible, the demarcation that separates the introspective method and its expansion into the biogenetic science from the behaviorist doctrine and its expansion into the psychology of behavior.

The evolutionally unfolded psyche is composed, in humans, of all conscious functions (thought, feelings, will) and extraconscious instances. The extraconscious, by definition, escapes introspection. The problem, therefore, is to know whether extraconscious productions—myths, dreams, and psychopathic symptoms—have a psychological meaning that can be disclosed. Conversely, no one can deny that one thinks, one is animated by feelings that vary from satisfaction to dissatisfaction, and one elaborates volitions in one's inner self. *Whether one wants it or not, one can know this only through introspection.*

The ill-fated error consists of failing to recognize the relationship between the inner nature of the psyche and the outer nature of the world. Therefore, it is important to emphasize strongly that there is no extension without intention (an immanent energetic tension).

Psychic life is not extensive or quantitative. It is intensive and qualitative. *What evolves psychically is the quality of intensity.* Along with the psychic intensity, the extended factor that is spatial extension also evolves by way of interinfluence.

The most elementary psychic quality is necessarily the most generalized form, the least differentiated of the interinfluence between the intensive and extensive (subject/object, psyche/world): *the excitability.*

These premises incur a consequence of primary significance for the study of evolution. The purely quantitative extended factor, the inert matter, does not exist. The atom already is animated with prelife, the intensity of which has not yet reached the degree of excitable vitality. The atom is an organism: It is penetrated with an immanent organizing spirit. What we call "inert matter" (a dead twig, a stone) is truly a set of highly organized atoms and molecules. The apparent inertia is due to the fact that the atoms and molecules form only a conglomerate. They do not constitute a harmoniously organized whole, submitted to the economic principle of division of work (immanent finalism).

Matter that became excitable through evolution, such as the cell, is not, like the atom, animated with prelife, but with manifest life. It is an animalized organism. The methodological principle of the genetic study of the excitable psyche consists of developing from the excitability, the psychic manifestation par excellence, the differentiations and integrations evolutionally and analogically determined by the constant interinfluence between the extensive world and intensive life.

The excitability, by being intensified evolutionally into anxiety or joy, leads to the generation of the human psyche, where the psychic intensity becomes a motivating intentionality that is superconsciously called upon to continue the evolutionary way, and subconsciously deflected toward psychopathic involutions.

NOTES

1. Translator's note: *Objectal* is relative to objects independent of the subject's ego; there is no English equivalent.

PART II

Anxiety
and Evolution

4

The Evolutionary and Involutionary Forms of Anxiety

A. THE EXCITANT AND THE EXCITABLE

Excitability is vital restlessness or anxiety that has not yet been differentiated. Excitability explains all vital manifestations, because its counterpole is the reactivity that strives to appease restlessness. Provided evolution is taken as a special form of reactivity, it can be explained generally, as well as in detail, by excitability insofar as the details are essential and not accidental.

"Animation" is in itself inexplicable, but is bipolarized by the psychic modalities of excitability and reactivity. All evolved modalities of the psyche are generated by excitability, the principle of restlessness, or, in other words, by reactivity that seeks satisfaction. The most primitive as well as the most evolved modalities of psychic functioning are analogically linked because they retain a common finalism: the satisfactory preservation of life. In view of a satisfactory survival, life endeavors to overcome restlessness by means of a constant evolutionary variation of the reactivity. The inexplicable urge to preserve vitality (the elementary need for survival) and its manifest means of reactive excitability, or conversely excitable reactivity, constitutes *immanent finalism*, which is evolutionary dynamism.

The animating restlessness manifests as driving appetites. Each living being is prompted by a stimulating hunger, the objective of which is attained only through reactivity since it is in the environmental world outside the subject. Because the objective of the original drive (hunger) is located outside the excitable psyche, the subject depends upon the environment. He is "driven" into it to seek the quieting of his excitability; the world becomes a source of multiple and external excitements that must be considered subordinate to *the primary excitability that occurs from an internal source.* Is it not mysterious that the world, despite its apparent independence from the subject, is constituted in such a manner that the subject's appetite finds in it the objects of its satisfaction? This complementarity would be impossible if the world were not mysteriously preadapted to the appetite that animates the subject, and if an evolutionary differentiation of the objectal world were not corresponding to each degree of evolutionary differentiation of the subject and his appetite.

*   *   *

Due to this indispensable reference to the material world, excitability is inevitably tied to materiality and the soma. It is a somatic as much as a psychic phenomenon. Because of its materialization, excitability or pure restlessness—the inexplicable principle of animation—potentially contains its own concrete manifestation: the psychosomatic excitation or the stimulation that has multiple forms and is conditioned and codetermined by the environmental world. Manifest excitation is produced through the soma and only with the help of the soma can it be discharged as a reaction toward the world.

The wisdom of language conveys these relationships: The excitation is the citation to externalize oneself. The citation that proceeds from the outer, from the world, is addressed to the psyche, which is perceived, through a spatial image, as if positioned within the soma. The psychic shock or the excitation cannot happen without the existence of an *outer excitant*, the world, and an *excitable inner*, the psyche.

The purely mechanical shock only exerts a *pressure*. It prompts the shifting of the inert object, its distortion and possibly even its destruction. Conversely, the psychic shock yields an *impression*. The successive excitations are impregnated in living matter.

When the outer motion, because of unfavorable environmental conditions, does not successfully satisfy the driving appetite, eventually the emotional impression will seek its reactive expression despite the suspension of satisfaction. This expression of the inexplicable animation triggers the evolutionary transformation of the psycho-somatic organism. The evolutionary reactivity is determined by emotions and the accumulation of emotions is determined by past frustration. The entire reactive behavior, evolution included, is strictly deter-

mined. However, the internalized and accumulated determinant factors cause the living matter to vary the reactive expressions of the
soma suitably and evolutionally, and therefore vary the somatic organization itself. We'll subsequently specify in detail this preliminary
statement of the immanent finalism that governs evolutionary phenomena.

The reactivity of the animated being implies an autonomous
finalism that bestows upon him a characteristic of freedom, despite
persisting determination. Evolution moves toward progressive liberation from environmental determination. Determination, which is apparently automatic and blind in the animal, evolutionally becomes
intentional and foreseeing in humans, where the emotivity is transformed into motivity, an intrapsychic causation of reactivity that becomes a voluntary activity. The activity, even though determined by
motives, becomes freely willed insofar as the motives conform to the
evolutionary meaning of life. Excitability in the pure state (immaterial
animation) exists no more than materiality in the pure state (material inertia).

Excitability originally materializes—or becomes existent—at the
most primitive level of life, in unicellular life forms, some of which possess an astoundingly differentiated sensitivity and a psychosomatic
functioning that, as Jennings demonstrated, by far exceeds the primitive reactions of tropism, described by Loeb. This does not prevent the
ancestor of unicellular life forms, which perhaps no longer exists, from
having been a rudimentary cell that was animated by an almost undifferentiated excitability.

*Evidently, the unicellular life form is a soma in our eyes and an
excitability in its own perception.* Similarly, we are also a soma for
others and more an excitability in our own perception. In order to
glimpse the nature of the manifest animation of the unicellular—the
seed of life—we must find the links that connect it to the evolved excitability of the human psyche.

However, the explanatory method should not simply satisfy itself
with a few vague analogies. It should uncover one by one from the undifferentiated reactivity of the primitive cell all the evolved functions
that have not yet unfolded. Only by doing so can we demonstrate that
knowledge can encompass all life phenomena from the most primitive
to the most evolved: the human being.

*   *   *

We perceive the seed of life as a cell composed of protoplasm, with a nucleus and a membrane. Protected by the membrane, living matter is enclosed in itself and separated from the environment. It is an indivisible unit, an individual.

The analogical comparison that is the sole means of reflection about life and its meaning permits us to say that primitive individuation and its elementary need for preservation is the seed of egoism that is a characteristic of every life, but that is bipolarized in humans as either the restrictive and pathogenic egocentricity or the free communication with the environment—a condition of health.

This polarization is already indicated in the primitive cell, because the membrane is not simply an organ of separation. It also performs the function of union with the environment and osmotically maintains an exchange of substances with it. The cell incorporates the substances that are favorable to its survival; the osmosis is selective.

The influx of toxic substances triggers a defense reflex. The pores of the membrane shrink and close. The cell is alive as long as this reaction, which surpasses the chemism of osmosi, is maintained. When its selective excitability, the only sign of life, disappears, it becomes merely chemical matter, a dead cell. Vital selectivity, which is still a pure reflex reaction, already prefigures the aptitude for a consciously guided choice or desire that, though infinitely more differentiated, has, nonetheless, lost the sureness of reflex. The half-affectively blind, half-consciously foreseeing desire, may prefer unhealthy excitation—this causes all the complications of human life.

Selective osmosis, which is the most primitive reflex reaction, prefigures more than nutrition. The cell feeds itself and splits in two. Bipartition is the first indication of reproduction. *Cell division is the unique exception to egoist indivisibility. In the course of evolution, the polarization of egoism toward lovingness very clearly manifests in the realm of reproduction.* It would be difficult to decide whether the cell feeds itself into order to bipart, or biparts in order to feed itself better. The two elementary drives, nutrition and reproduction, are originally undifferentiated. Neither prevails. Their common root is the need to survive. Nutrition assures individual survival and reproduction assures species survival. Evolution, in fact, has the characteristic of an elementary drive. Evolutionary drive is a special case of the need for preservation. Indeed, between appetite and environment, there is a modal preadaptation that issues from the inexplicable animation. This preadaptation, however, is accidentally modifiable and more or less adequate for species survival. The restlessness of appetite manifests in vital anxiety, which is overcome only by a constant effort of evolutionary readaptation.

Nutritional selectivity and presexual bipartition are not the only drive phenomena that distinguish living matter from the prevital chemism of supposedly inert matter. The cell is far from being a mere mechano-chemical automatism; it is endowed with an *evolutionary drive*; otherwise, only unicellular life forms would exist today. Evolutionary growth can be called "spiritual drive" because the most efficient means of orientation is to prospect, at first perceptively and eventually cognitively. The evolution of the primitive cell produces the *manifestation of species* that have a more complex organization.

In certain cases, the basic need to survive favors *a grouping of the cells* that multiplied through bipartition. The evolutionary plasticity of live matter contains the potential for such colonies to be transformed into multicellular organisms by the division of work. Groups of cells specialize and transform into organs, which become exclusively responsible for either the nutritive or the reproductive function. In turn, the reproductive organs differentiate into sexed forms (male and female); this process was designed at a more primitive level, where bipartition is often accomplished after the passing union of two cells that mutually fecundate by exchanging their nuclei. Through the division of work, all cells bequeath their sensitivity to the nervous cell. The nervous system is responsible for communicating with the environment by collecting excitations and arranging reactions.

When they appeared, multicellular creatures were not equipped with perceptive organs. The search for the favored excitant and escape from the toxic excitant were still very primitively and automatically exercised by trial and error. Locomotion was passive and the organs of locomotion were often barely indicated. In an aquatic environment, for instance, multicellular individuals are transported by the current, unless they happen to settle in locations favorable to survival.

These two methods of providing for vital needs—fixation to the ground or passive and random movement—are vitally significant for species evolution. They eventually differentiate plant life from animal life. The differentiation is accomplished by the adaptation to extraaquatic life conditions. The plant takes root in the earth, drawing up its food. It will evolve into forms ever better adapted to this primitive condition of existence.

Conversely, aquatic and land animals that must strive for survival through motion are more prone to vital restlessness and its embodiment as the anxiety of dissatisfaction. The evolutionary dynamism of anxiety differentiates the appetites of drives and their means of satisfaction.

Gradually, the primitive method of orientation by trial and error is replaced by an orientation of perceiving distance. In order to perform its function of preservation successfully, it needs an autonomous means of transportation. The structure of the organism is no longer determined only by the drive organs (the digestive tract and sexual apparatus), but also by the position of the limbs and, especially, as the evolutionary development progresses, by the spine and cranium, which provide the core for the vital centers of the nervous system.

These somatic organs, however, remain in the service of appetite and its elementary need for satisfaction, which are both psychic phenomena. The organs are the externalized and instrumental aspects of the intentional and finalist psychic function that governs their functioning and defines life. For each degree of differentiation of the organic instrument, there is a corresponding intensified psychic sensitivity, with its emotional nuances of satisfaction and dissatisfaction in relation to the world, which is itself evolutionally created by perceptivity. In this complex evolution, the unilateral relation of cause and effect does not exist. The cause (whether psychic, somatic, or environmental) creates the effect and the effect again becomes the cause. *The psyche and the soma with the environment constitute a functional unit: evolving life.*

*   *   *

The fundamental significance of the reflex reaction did not escape physiologists. They proposed explanatory systems based upon this very primitive reactional mode, while putting aside the central phenomenon of excitability, in the hope they could achieve a synthesis that would point to the prevalence of organic phenomena and their physiological study.

Even nature seems to indicate this prevalence; indeed, in evolved organisms, the flux of excitation is constrained to move along the organic paths prescribed by the nervous system. The reactive discharge is organized step by step by the shift of synapses and their chronaxic regulation; it is a very complicated organic layout that, because of its excessive complexity, is controlled by a central organ, the brain. One cannot remain unimpressed or underestimate the importance of the organic when contemplating the existence of genuine arc reflexes and their subcortical points of localization that, when experimentally excited, initiate an entire cascade of reflexes, the coordinated automat-

ism of which provokes the characteristic attack or escape behavior of a
given species, even to the mimic expression of the emotion. However,
we should not conclude that the importance of the organic factor is
preponderant. Similar experiments could never provoke, and reflexology—even Pavlov's theory, despite his signalization theory—could
never successfully explain the higher forms of the reactive discharge
that are intentionally controllable and individually adaptable to the
variable circumstances of the environment. The triumph of organicist
reflexology would have been complete, if it could have demonstrated—
as it attempted—that these higher individual reactions of a more or
less conscious character are localized in the circumscribed zones of the
nervous system. We know of the complete failure of these attempts.

This decisive failure impelled a revision of the entire problem.
The whole organism reacts to each excitation. The physiological explanation should take care to establish a synthesis that can account for
the structuralization that organizes the preparatory stages of the final
reaction into a *whole*. Thus, the reflexes triggered in cascades lose their
predominant importance and even their automatic character. They
lose their significance in a whole that imposes its finality instead of
forming a conglomerate of particularities. Unfortunately, the psyche is
again carefully eliminated from the total reactivity of the psychosomatic organism.

The totality conceived so far concerns only somatic relations with
the environment—the reactive situation. It does not consider the true
totality, which should include the inner cause of the reactivity—psychic excitability. Isn't the Gestalt, which is presented as a result of the
formatory power that is exercised on the soma because of the need to
safeguard the reactive unity, the product of psychic finalism, of a
preconscious organizing spirit at work in everything existing?

The formatory power of evolutionary finalism tends toward psychosomatic structuralizations that are more differentiated but better
integrated and harmonized. Evolution creates ever more potent functional harmonies that are, therefore, more sensitized. The power of
harmony exists as a function of the increasing number of excitations
to be integrated and organized into a functional whole; in turn, the
progressive sensitization depends upon the multiplication of objectal
excitations, each of which provokes a transitory disturbance of the
inner harmony (which is total only in the moments when the appetites
are assuaged and, moreover, when the environment lacks any disturbing threat).

In higher animals, the reflex arcs form a whole that is bound into a nervous system that is the organic instrument of the instinctive foresight of preconsciousness. The various forms of instinctivity that trigger the somatic reactions of hunt and escape denote, by their surprising ingenuousness, an underlying psychic factor, a kind of fore-knowledge of environmental conditions. However, this preconsciousness is still fully incorporated, "incarnated." Psyche and soma form a quasi-indistinct whole. The physiological structure still masks the underlying psychic functioning that clearly appears only in humans where reflex becomes reflection, while the instinctivity of pre-conscious psychosomatic harmony evolves toward the demand of superconscious self-harmonization. At the human level, instinctive intentionality is differentiated into a multitude of motivating intentions that deliberating reflection, which is superconsciously guided, tends to reintegrate and synthesize into a harmonious whole; otherwise they become a pathogenic failure. The eventuality of essential failure is the primary cause of human anxiety. It first concerns the excess of the differentiation of motives, which is the insufficiently harmonious reintegration. But in fact the evolutionally formatory and transfor- mational power of anxiety is bound to this essential cause. Because it is difficult to attain the perfect form of the harmony of intentions, the human evolutionary aim becomes a superconsciously directive ideal that is a biologically founded ethical imperative.

*   *   *

These still very general considerations that concern the relation between the evolution of reflex reaction and the psychic formatory principle result in an important observation:

> *The concrete obstacle transforms immanent restlessness*
> *(vital energy) into anxiety. Obstacle and anxiety form a*
> *polar couple; and it is between the environmental pole*
> *(obstacle) and the psychic pole (anxiety) that the*
> *energetic exchanges (through the soma) that constitute*
> *evolutionary dynamism are accomplished.*

Thus, anxiety becomes an integration of the obstacle as a memorial trace. The anxiety-laden obstacle integration disturbs the equilibrium of the situation being experienced, which is indissolubly formed by the triad of "psyche-soma-environment." This disturbance is overcome only by evolutionary readaptation that concerns soma, psyche, and environment. The differentiation of the psychophysical organism can be accomplished only by a memorial integration of the ex-

citant environment. The memorial integration of the environment has
always been spiritualizing. *Evolutionary integration leans toward material possessiveness and also toward a possessiveness that is spiritually cognitive of the environment. The integral psychic representation of
the environment-obstacle is the higher means of orientation. It alone
can remove the characteristic of anxiety from the evolutionary differentiation between environment and organism.*

The spiritualizing aspect of memorial integration is inseparable
from the sublimating character that engineers the metamorphosis of
anxiety into lovingness.

The highly differentiated functions of the human psyche that are
regulated by intentionality remain under the law of integration. The
almost unlimited potential of diversification of activity modes should
be controlled by a voluntary form of integration: the effort to reunify
desires harmoniously, the condition of joy. The anxietude opposed to joy
is defined as a transitory loss or, in the event of morbidity, as the
progressive destruction of the harmonious unity (which follows an excessive differentiation of the vital need into insufficiently controlled
multiple desires). In this light, *anxiety occurs as an infraction of the
evolutionary law.*

The law of differentiation-integration can be called the "preconscious spirit" that governs the psychosomatic organization of living
matter. Because of the analogical unity of evolutionary unfolding, the
law responsible for the unity even governs the functioning of the
theoretical spirit in which the differentiation-integration manifests in
the form of the "analysis-synthesis" polarity. (It is no formal analogy to
recall that the multicellular organism, subject to heredity, is always
newly reconstituted from the ovule by way of progressive bipartition,
which is a special case of differentiation-integration.)

The interplay of these two polar modes of evolutionary reactivity
(differentiation-integration) constitutes the *law that rules the analogical unfolding of evolution.*

*   *   *

The last statement is a comprehensive view of the lawfulness that
binds the lower to the higher (reflex to reflection) and causes *evolving
life to remain a structured whole.* Evolutionary structuralization concerns more than psychosomatic organization. Species can be considered as "islands" that emerge from the lawful immensity, and their
sporadic emergence is due to the codetermining influence of the accidental factor in the environment.

The previous conclusion about the evolutionary law permits the discovery of various *concrete processes* that activate the modes of evolutionary reactivity from reflex reaction.

The absence of the excitant of nutrition suspends the
reflex reaction.

As the satisfying reaction no longer responds immediately to the animating excitability called hunger, the anxiety-laden dissatisfaction is prolonged and accumulates in the intrapsyche.

A retention of excitation: The memorial integration of
the coveted object or of the anxiety-laden obstacle
corresponds to a suspended reaction.

Within the time span of the retention, the energetic exchange actually occurs between the two internalized poles of the dislocated reflex, rather than between the environment and the individual. An intrapsychic "motion" manifests, an emotion that is the energetic seed of psychic evolution, in the place of the *motor reaction*.

The retention, with the impatience due to internalized, dissatisfied excitation, can be viewed as a kind of emotional "presentation" of the missing object, because of its nuance of avidity (the seed of desire); in humans, this leads to re-presentation, the faculty of representing the missing object emotionally as well as imaginatively or cognitively. Retentional excitability is more originally characteristic of the living organism than perceptive excitability, one of its evolutionary consequences. Perceptive excitability, unlike retentional covetousness, concerns a spatial distance, rather than a temporal distension. The emergence of the perceptive organs brings about the evolution of the emotional presentation of the missing excitant to the degree, even if weak, of a figurative representation of a perceptively known object that is absent at the present time. The memorial presentation of the missing object cannot be separated from the organic perception; it is its psychic condition of selective *perceptivity*—the capacity to translate what is perceived as a function of its value of satisfaction. Without the psychic quality of valuating apprehension, the sensory organs would be useless, for they would not successfully delineate the desired object from the (otherwise) undifferentiated chaos of stimuli. *Memorial retention is the first degree of evolutionary differentiation.* Already, the primitive being unconsciously "valuates" as a result of the selective appetite. The absence of the favorite excitant stimulates the preferential valuation by holding the satisfaction in a retentional suspension. The absent excitant, which is memorially integrated, sharpens the vague *expectation* until it eventually becomes the capacity of *attention*.[1]

However, the dissociation of the primitive reflex into internalized excitation and suspended reaction not only produces psychic results. An absent nutrition excitant provokes a psychic effect and a purely organic sensation of extended hunger as well. The fact that psychic and somatic effect go together is a property of the psychosomatic organism; their common cause is the animating appetite. Extended privations that are re-activated throughout generations create new reactive modes that are inefficient without the complementary somatic modification. The work of the retentional energy would be uselessly modifying the psychic functioning if the forms of higher reactivity it was elaborating were powerless to organize the soma-matter with the aim of creating organs of active discharge. Conversely, the evolutionary emergence of organs (which can more easily be observed) would have no meaningful or efficient finalism without the complementary evolution of the psychic function that animates them. Psychic restlessness and physiological hunger must necessarily complete each other in order to produce evolutionary appeasement in the event of an extended privation. Either the physiological form of appetite ties itself to other excitants that are more easily attainable or the purely emotional valuation, rather than changing its objective, successfully elucidates the nature of the obstacle, which is then integrated as anxiety-laden envy. New modes of satisfying discharge are thus created, equipped with their executive organs.

The simultaneity of psychic and organic transformations is the cardinal problem of evolution. Nothing is explained if its solution remains undiscovered. The retention is the energetic drive of evolution because it differentiates reflex and emotionally, imaginatively, or cognitively integrates the environment. This is an evolutionary process from its emotional beginning because it is prone to extend throughout generations and is therefore hereditary accumulation. Retention creates both the transformational dynamism of anxiety and the finalism that ceaselessly attempts to overcome it. By the creation of more refined organs, the evolutionary differentiation of the psychophysical organism differentiates the perceived environment and leads to a clarified perception of the favorite objects and, also, to the differentiated perception of the environment and therefore to the encounter of new obstacles. Excitations are more frequently retained, reactions are suspended, and, in the interval between excitation and reaction, the dissatisfied tension of anxiety-laden envy is accumulated and eventually demands an evolutionary discharge. A *constant intensification of retentional energy* results. The process of retention, once started, amplifies and gradually creates a more evolved species.

* * *

These conclusions invite the review of the interpretation of Pavlov's experiment that led to the organicist hypothesis of evolution, which is, by far, the most coherent. It is truly an experiment of retention.

Pavlov's experiment is inadequately interpreted if the attention is placed only upon the dramatic aspect of the physiological reaction and if the psychic phenomenon of retention, which was provoked by the impossibility of reaching the excitant rather than by its absence, is neglected. The bait, displayed from a distance, does not trigger a mechanical shock or a chemical reaction, but a vital response of the whole organism. To believe that this physiological reaction could manifest without its indispensable psychic complement is to misunderstand gravely the nature of vital phenomena. In the experiment, two psychic factors come into play: the *driving appetite*, an emotionally exalted factor (following the retention of the excitation and the suspension of the satisfying reaction) without which the unconditioned reflex of gastric secretion could not be produced, and the *associative imagination*, without which the conditioning of the reflex through the sound of the bell would be impossible.

The psychic factor (conditionability) genetically precedes conditioning and therefore cannot be its epiphenomenal consequence. Even "unconditioned" reflexes are evolutionarily conditioned and, before the study of conditioned reflexes, we should establish the genesis of the so-called unconditioned reflex. Indeed, the term *unconditioned reflex* is formed by opposition to the term *conditioned reflex*. The intention of Pavlovian theory gives it yet another significance. The "unconditioned" has no conditions and therefore has no need for an explanation; furthermore, it is inexplicable. Indeed, so-called unconditioned reflexes cannot find an explanation if we deny their modal origin in a psychic as well as a somatic nature. By excluding the psyche, the inexplicable is introduced in existence to then be explained. The psychic phenomenon is therefore confused with the "inexplicable," which is characteristic of the materialist doctrine.

* * *

So, it is important to oppose the physiological hypothesis (which does not include a psychic modality for fear of being stranded in metaphy-

sics) with a hypothesis of evolution that avoids metaphysical speculation by acknowledging the inexplicable animation and attempts to incorporate the totality of the genetic modalities (psyche, soma, environment) by making the phenomenon of retention an exclusive basis—the
means to actualize the evolutionary law of differentiation-integration.

B. RETENTION

In this present exposition, it is impossible to develop the details of
either the evolutionary manifestations of retention or the transformational dynamism of anxiety (which is more or less the same).

It is necessary to *draw the outline of psychic evolution* that leads
from the monad to the beginning of the higher functions, including the
specific forms of human anxietude, as well as to the genesis of a retentional dynamism that can transform intensified anxiety into an intense feeling of vital satisfaction or joy.

Time and Space

Expectation derives from the most primitive form of retention; it
is the first indication of time and, correlatively, of space. Energetic tension, which is inserted between the retained excitation and the suspended reaction, is immediately felt as a time lag where restlessness
is poised for its own appeasement. *Time-expectation* is an *inner tension*
that is accompanied by *attention* and directed toward the outer obstacle. This attentive tension eventually transforms into a cognitive attention and a voluntary intention designed to arrange the multiplied
intentions or intrapsychic motives of future actions. Each evolutionary
stage of intention is accompanied by the evolution of spatial extension.

Since the evolutionary unfolding is a temporal phenomenon, it is
foreshadowed as a "seed" in the retentional expectation of the monad
(the term *seed*, as figurative as it may be, is the most fit to summarize
the evolutionary unfolding of life). Evolution is summarized by the fact
that the retentional expectation of the monad consists of patience as
much as impatience. In humans, the temporal retention splits into its
two factors of patience—the sublimative force—and the excess of impatience—a weakness that degrades the retained excitations into
pathogenic irritations.

The patience-impatience of expectation, which is the first intima-
tion of temporal perception, does not constitute a genuine temporal
continuum. Time is still fragmented. The individual lives only in the
moments where he is in a state of innerly prolonged excitation. Only

the emotional tension toward the absent and coveted excitant makes him *present to himself*. This still purely emotional and obscure fragmentary self-presence can, nevertheless, be viewed as the seed of a constant presence—the conscious that will evolve to be the "presence of mind." Due to the absence of a quieting object, the primitive self-presence tears apart the preadaptation between subject and object and transforms animation, which is the potential principle of life, into concrete life. The perception of the objectal environment remains as vague as the self-perception, although the first stage of objectal attention that will eventually divide the still undifferentiated environment into distinct objects begins to correspond to the emotional expectation of the subject, in the course of evolution. Each moment of self-presence vanishes at the point of satisfaction, when subject and object reunite. Liberated from the distressing duality that is the condition of life and existence, the subject fades into a quietude that transitorily reestablishes a "nonexistence" from which life is barely emerging.

Each experienced timespan leaves its imprint of awakened restlessness; these successive imprints eventually prevent the return to the initial quietude where vital functions drowse. The fragmentary lags of retained excitation and impatient expectation thus begin gradually to follow one another and link into a chain of quasi-uninterrupted vitality. They stimulate the subject to live by subjecting him more and more to an uninterrupted stream of excitations.

Exist means *ex-sistere*, to be outside, to be expelled (from the mystery into space-time). This progressive expulsion is evolutionary life.

(A final return to quietude is the ineluctable end of individual life. Insofar as individuation evolves toward consciousness, definitive quieting, death, is anxiously dreaded. During his entire "restless" existence, the individual could not survive if he were not to draw his force to live from the periodic return to quietude that is sleep.)

The stream of excitations intensifies emotivity, the indication of life, and this intensification, due to the combination of fragmentary experiences of restlessness, forces the living being, who has been progressively expelled from quietude, to intensify his vital reaction, seeking quietude in the evolutionary adaptation to the conditions of existence rather than in a return to nonexistence. The conditioned and conditioning environment acquires, insofar as the individual becomes temporal by expectation, the complementary characteristic of a spatial extension. Nevertheless, space doesn't possess a dimension of depth (which appears only with the perception of distance) and is not yet dimensional in past and future. Space still adheres, so to speak, to the membrane in the form of tactile and gustatory sensations that are pleasing or displeasing according to whether they are favorable or unfavorable to survival. These sensations, which are projected into the countermanifestation of the environment, differentiate it into preferred or avoided locations that can then be used as reference points.

Passive expectation, by becoming reactive attention, detects the temporal modifications of the environment. As the retained excitations fuse into a continual emotivity, the expectation eventually constitutes the temporal continuum, which, at the human level, becomes a condition of causal exploration of the spatial continuum.

*   *   *

Originally, the psychic restlessness of a dissatisfied appetite, or the retentional phenomenon manifests in the soma as a convulsive innervation that is contractile and retractile. Used for wriggling motion, it is not only a means of locomotion, but an attempt to grope for orientation. The inevitable errors of this primitive method of orientation have, in turn, a favorable repercussion upon the evolution of the nascent psyche; they gradually shape the tendency to circumvent errors—a rough model of a primitive capacity to learn by experience.

The adaptive modifications just indicated are based upon the definition of the evolutionary process. *Intentional finalism* attempts to reestablish the unity of origin of the individual and his differentiated environment, so that the individual remains nutritionally integrated in the variable conditions of his environment. *As harmony is unity in complexity*, the law of evolution imposes a progressive organopsychic differentiation and a harmonious reintegration of the differentiated organism in the universe, which itself is also more and more differentiated. Only those species that evolutionally attain the harmonizing reunion will successfully survive.

As the psychic quality of excitable emotivity is the condition of perceiving an excitant world, the subject, as it moves, creates around itself the objectal world, its countermanifestation, which unfolds into distinct objects. These multiple objects that emerge from what is undifferentiated become, in turn, multiple and variable excitations that are the cause of somatic reactivity that is increasingly guided, differentiated, and intensified by the complementary unfolding of perceptivity. (For instance, the primitively perceived glimmer, by gradually sensitizing the receptive membrane, will eventually be perceived as the solar light that radiates over a world filled with distinct objects.)

Apart from these evolutionary modalities, a *mysterious preadaptation is manifest by the fact that from the origin and throughout evolution, the outer world offers to inner life, or to appetites, the satisfactory conditions of survival*. Preadaptation is the *essential condition* of the multiple accidental adaptations (due to unfavorable accidents of the environment). Throughout all evolutionary modifications, preadaptation or adaptability remains the immutable condition of survival; it links all the stages of evolution, as differentiated as they may be, into an analogically unfolded unity. It is the *immanent* finalism, the unexplainable animating force or the *vital force*.

Preadaptation is not occult; it is mysterious. The mechanistic error is the desire to explain the mysterious preadaptation—the aptitude to live and evolve—using the occult notion of absolute matter. Moreover, materialism, like spiritualism, pretends to deny the necessary preadaptation, while it introduced it—as we proved—in the occult form of a preestablished time/space framework. In that way, they deprive themselves of the possibility of glimpsing the retention phenomenon and its result: evolution, which includes psyche, soma, and environment.

Preconscious Memory

Retention possesses a *memorial characteristic that concerns the individual as well as generations*. The constancy of common privations for individuals of a given species becomes the cause of a retention in a specific direction. The retentional energy works for all individuals of the species in a determined direction, and this inner work necessarily extends throughout generations insofar as the specific privations persist. Memorial imprints of a specific, common, and constant direction are retained and accumulated throughout generations without producing any observable effect until vital restlessness, by mobilizing them to its advantage, eventually succeeds in provoking an adaptive mutation, if only in a few individuals who, henceforth better armed against the common frustration, have an increased chance of survival and, thereby, of reproduction as well.

Memorial retention permits us to understand of the crucial phenomenon of evolution, *the hereditarily acquired adaptation*. Evolution is impossible without acquiring *higher psychic qualities*. Materialist theories vainly endeavor to explain evolution from an acquired adaptation that is exclusively organic. This obvious error led to Weissman's hypothesis, currently in vogue, that expresses that evolution is not due to any acquisition, but to random variations that operate within the chromosomes and genes and that therefore become hereditary. But, rather than explaining the observable phenomenon of evolutionary finalism, this randomness risks producing a profusion of nonviable monstrosities.

Only the psychic qualities of animating appetite and memorial retention permit understanding of the scope of the evolutionary phenomenon that includes psyche, soma, and environment. *Retention accumulates the acquisitions that are codetermined by environmental obstacles without any immediate profit, and animating restlessness, the transformational dynamism of anxiety, mobilizes them in its evolutionary aim of appeasement.*

                              *   *   *

We should distinguish between a memorial retention that is prolonged throughout generations, at the expense of multiple suffering, and *heredity*, which transmits the acquisitions mobilized by the liberating finalism of anxiety, and makes them the adaptive acquired ability of the species. The *hereditary memory* that stabilizes *species* can be added to the *retentional memory* that modifies individuals throughout generations.

The organs of individual memory is the nervous system and the brain. The organs of memory of the species are genes and chromosomes. Originally, the memory of the species (heredity) is not really different from the individual's memory of retention. The bipartition obviously transmits to each new cell the psychosomatic acquisitions.

The whole organism of the multicellular creatures that became bisexed bears the mark of the sex; that proves the perseverance of the formatory influence of germinal cells that have become the carriers of hereditary memory. The act of fecundation gives birth to a new organism that can unfold, in the course of its maturation, the acquired adaptation of the species and accumulate, in turn, new retentional acquisitions hereditarily transmittable (provided they concern the totalitarian vitality of the psychosomatic organism).

Only the comprehension of the process of psychogenic retention allows for a clear discernment of the two forms of preconscious memory (generally confused by the improper term *organic memory*). Retention and heredity are forms of "memory" because they contain a *recollection of the environment*. This recollection is, for individual retention, the emotional "presentation" of the absent excitant and, for heredity, the psychosomatic totality of acquired adaptations.

There is no purely organic memory. From the beginning, memory has been organopsychic, and from its psychic components higher forms (imaginative and cognitive) of conscious memory emerge.

* * *

Instinct

The multicellular organism eventually outgrows the stage of primitive tactile perception, in which orientation and movement happen by a convulsive groping that is often liable to error. As memorial retention progressively organizes time and space into an emotionally experienced *continuum*, the shifting motions that are oriented by distance perception and emotional tension—now continual attention—begin to acquire a character of adaptive precision. They are polarized into attack and escape. This polar couple of emotional reactivity is the first manifestation of instinct in the service of animating appetite. Attack and escape retain, because of the suddenness of the fury or fear trigger, the primitively convulsive character of vital restlessness. The randomness of groping and its possibility for error are evolutionally replaced by a more advanced degree of objectal recognition, for these convulsed movements of attack and escape are directed by selective emotions of attraction and repulsion that recall the sureness of the primitive reflex reaction.

Elementary instinctivity participates in the unfathomable depth of existence. To know the prey or the mortal enemy is not an exclusive result of adaptation, but the effect of a mysterious foreknowledge.[2] Just like the drives it serves, instinctive foreknowledge proves to be partially rooted in the inexplicable sphere of the subject's preadaptation to the object and retains the characteristic of primitive selectivity in relation to the preferred or harmful excitant. This does not prevent elementary instinctivity of attack and escape from being an adaptive acquisition. Consequently, attack and escape become the characteristics of either division of carnivorous or herbivorous animals.

The mysterious preadaptation concerns the selective sureness of instinct. Adaptation, on the other hand, due to retentional energy and its hereditary memory, generates various means of attack or defense that rapidly develop the characteristic traits of the behavior of any given species and also of its somatic organization, determined by the organs of execution. Nonetheless, the adaptive functioning of secondary instinct remains impregnated with the preadapted sureness of elementary instinctivity.

The preadapted selectivity and the acquired adaptation that specializes it into instinctivity succeed only in creating an *overall orientation*, at the level of foreseeing consciousness. The environment is not yet differentiated into objects that would be conceived as independently existing from the subject. Even in higher animals, the object often is not located in its resting state but uniquely by its shifting movement, which alerts the emotional attention used in stalking the prey or in watching for danger. (However, it is true that the sense of smell can replace this perceptive insufficiency.) Even at that, instinctive foreknowledge does not discern the enemy, or the prey, such as we perceive it, but only some traits that have been designed for use as warning signals. This partial and subjective perception constitutes the "overall situation" in which the excitant and the excited are united and that determines their reciprocal behavior. (An artificial trap, for instance, when it does not present the instinctively foreknown traits—even if it imitates as perfectly as possible the mortal enemy of the species—will not provoke any reaction, while the presence of the foreknown trait activates a reaction, even if the trap itself as a whole only approximately imitates the actual enemy.) The eventuality of even fatal errors corresponds to the sureness of preadapted selectivity because of the rigid overall aspect of instinctive adaptation.

Evolutionary dynamism of anxiety tends to overcome the overall aspect of instinctivity by evolving toward the flexibility of the semiconscious choice of humans (already vaguely prefigured in anthropoids). This new evolutionary step cannot be accomplished without the differentiation of instinctivity into a nuanced multitude of anxieties and without the differentiation of "appetite" into a multitude of desires. The explosion of instinctivity into multiple desires and anxieties is the decisive step leading toward hominization. The desire, in its human form, is constrained to meditate its future satisfactory externalization.

Desire and Anxiety

The most evolved stage of animal life is instinctivity as it becomes intellectualized in higher mammals. Their desires, nevertheless, remain little differentiated. The promises of satisfaction, barely individualized, are uniformly incorporated into the elementary vital need of the driving appetites without the possibility of meaningless exaltation. As for anxiety, it still is a vague restlessness, barely distinguishable from the fear caused by a present danger.

Desires and anxieties, properly speaking, are exclusively human feelings that are individually nuanced and that can be multiplied to the extent of meaninglessly exceeding the natural demand of driving appetites. However, the tonality of pleasure and displeasure, of satisfaction and dissatisfaction, in various degrees of intensity, is the link of appetites common to animal and human. It is, therefore, analogically justified to include in a common denominator all the phenomena of excitability; since the beginning, restlessness of appetites manifests as "anxiety-laden desire."

Even in a primitive form, retention differentiates anxiety-laden desire in its two components: the retained excitation prefigures anxiety and the suspended primitive reaction signifies desire. In instinct, desire and anxiety are more specified, linked as they are to attack and escape. The differentiation into nuanced feelings can operate only as the instinctive alert triggered by stereotyped signals is replaced by a *figurative foresight* of satisfying or dissatisfying environmental conditions. The imaginative character is the characteristic trait of human desires and anxieties. However, imaginative foresight is prefigured in the stereotyped foreknowledge of instinct: typical signals, to be capable of identifying the attractive or dangerous nature of stimulus, must already contain, if not an objectal image, at least the image of one or many invariably distinctive traits.

The image, as it becomes specified, multiplied, and fixed, not only serves to identify the present stimulus; *it also represents the missing object.* Thus becoming a *purely intrapsychic stimulus* and a support of foresight, imagination replaces instinctive foresight. *Perceptive and momentary fear is being differentiated into a multitude of feelings that eventually constitute the imaginative anxiety of humans.*

Imagination or the internalized image of the world is an evolved form of retention and its memorial trace. The imaginative foresight of the future possibilities of discharges and their satisfactions places a barrier between animal and human life that is as great as the one separating the animal from the plant form.

Despite this fundamental difference between human and animal, human life remains perfectly integrated in the evolutionary law and its immanent direction, which is common to all forms of life and founded on the transformational power of anxiety: The history of the animal realm is characterized by the advent of the perceptive apparatus, allowing orientation in space. With the advent of humankind, *orientation in time* is added to orientation in space.

The animal lives in the here and now, but humans do not live only in the present; their retentional memory extends from past to future. A human knows he is the same as the one who lived yesterday and that his life will be prolonged tomorrow. He is capable of imagining his life to come and of foreseeing the means of satisfactions. As time is differentiated in its dimensions and integrated into a continuum, the human draws from past experience and projects into the future. Imaginative foresight will evolve toward intellectual foresight and hence toward clear-sightedness of spirit.

All higher faculties of the thinking animal are the result of the retentional capacity to imagine a future life in view of a meaningful orientation; this which can, however, become meaningless because of the power of exaltation of imagination.

NOTES

1. Translator's note: In French, *attente* (expectation) *attention* (attention) have the same root.

2. The spider, for instance, weaves its web as if it knew perfectly the nature and the life conditions of its prey. The movements of the captured prey, by shaking the web, act as warning signals that automatically activate in the spider an entire cascade of reactions that compose the instinct of attack, adapted to the situation. The fly, however, as we perceive it, does not exist in the universe of the spider. The situation as it presents itself to the spider is totally inaccessible to us. By interpreting our own perception, we are forced to observe that everything is happening as if the behavior of the fly formed an indissoluble "whole" with the behavior of the spider, an organic unity; that is to say, the conditions of existence of the fly are imprinted—by inexplicable preadaptation—in the organism of the spider, in the psychosomatic organization in its totality! For what would be the use of the instinctive foreknowledge of the prey and its conditions of life if the soma of the spider were not equipped with the glands that secrete the thread to weave the web?

5

Anxiety at the Human Level

A. IMAGINATION AND COGNITION

The biogenetic consequence of imaginative prevision and its resulting multiplication of desires is the *expansion of drives*. At the human level, *the preconscious spiritual drive* (the evolutionary growth toward perceptive and eventually cognitive means of orientation) broadens the field of satisfactions. To spontaneously felt satisfaction and dissatisfactions, we can add foresight of future satisfactions, which, as they are only vaguely meditated in semilucidity, produce ill-established plans, the realization of which usually brings disappointment.

The expanded spiritual drive has the task of valuating promises lucidly in order to avoid disappointments. Meaningless or meaningful valuation generates a whole gamut of nuanced feelings that vary from anxiety to joy.

The need for valuation, a function of the spirit, extends to the multitude of material and sexual desires generated from the elementary drives of nutrition and reproduction.

Nutrition extends into the possibility of providing for material satisfactions from a process of preparatory work that can accomplish long-term projects and accumulate wealth, a process that has already led primitive societies to economic organization by the division of work.

Sexuality, when surpassing the transitory union through the act, raises itself to the level of a durable relationship of parents-partners who project their hopes for the child's future through an educational effort that is intended to transmit to the lineage the ancestrally acquired adaptation codified in customs, principles, and institutions.

*Human behavior cannot be understood if we are content to develop
it from animal drives or social relationships and not take into account
the biogenetic phenomenon of the expansion of drives, the cause of so-
ciability and socialization and also a cause of the danger of perversion.*

B. WILL AND THOUGHT

In the human psyche, retention becomes foreseeing and intentional.
Willed retention is characterized by an inversion of attention. The attention first concentrates on the intrapsychic situation created by the
multiplication of desires, instead of being first directed outwardly. The
evolutionary meaning of the reversal of attention into intention consists of exposing the conflict of multiple and contradictory desires to a
prolonged control, an *intrapsychic work* of intimate deliberation, in
order to dissolve indecision and elaborate decision. Thus, the automatic reactivity of the animal becomes, by intervention of voluntary control, *human activity.*

The overall situation that was created by instinctive foresight
could unite the animal to its environment, although in a still stereotyped way. This overall bond, which already became somewhat variable because of the appearance of a weak imaginative foresight, is to
become more differentiated. In the pursuit of evolution, *affective imagination becomes spiritualized into* a cognitive representation of the environmental universe. *The cognition differentiates the overall relation
with the environment. It conceptualizes images and thus provides the
will with its higher means of adaptation, as the reflection upon objectal
representations gradually discerns the causes and effects of environmental modifications.* The instinctive adaptation to a stereotyped environment metamorphoses into an ability for *flexible* adaptation and
can estimate and even foresee all the changes of a situation, thus plac-
ing the subject in a *time/space environment in which incessantly
changing objectives become distinct objects that exist independent of the
subject* and remain accessible to voluntary intervention, because of the
causal orientation.

C. CONSCIOUS LIFE

The faculties of thought and will cannot exist independently. Without
a causally foreseeing and selectively valuating thought, the will would
have no precise aim to attain; without the will of execution, thought
would be without a productive efficiency. *Thought and will* form a

couple; their energetic exchanges determine the *feelings* of satisfaction and dissatisfaction of the life that is now conscious of itself.

(Both voluntary and cognitive, the conscious spirit is the most evolved manifestation of vital phenomena; the result is that the principle underlying all phenomena—the animation, in itself inexplicable—can be modally described from the observable effect that is the genesis of species. Inexplicable animation, while it remains mysterious, manifests as *preconscious spirit, the organizer of the soma*, which is eventually revealed as the conscious spirit that both explains life and valuates desires, by way of evolutionary spiritualization.)

The spirit thus regulates intrapsychic life and growing complexities. (In the mythical image, the immanent spirit symbolically becomes the transcending Spirit that animates and regulates life.)

The ideal would be to arrange the differentiated and evolved psyche (its harmonizing integration). Individuals are differentiated in character because of voluntary retention. Everyone has a personal character, a favorite and particular tendency to react after deliberation.

As a part of society, the individual participates in the common intention, the aim of which is to organize the satisfaction of the vital need in order to guarantee everyone's survival as far as possible. The species no longer adapts to environmental conditions through organic mutation; *it adapts the environment to its needs* by technical interventions that are the result of conscious foresight. The social milieu, however, while protecting the individual against the perils of a direct environment (frequently fatal at the animal level), exposes him to a danger of a new order.

Each individual with his personal character becomes, in a manner of speaking, a species of his own. In this way, he is designed to evolve for himself and by himself. The individual is passively determined by the current constellation of the social milieu insofar as his intensity of animation is weak and insofar as he refers to conventions and not to his own animating appetite, which can be called, because of the demand for satisfaction, *evolutionary egoism, and which is opposed to egocentric stagnation and social conventionalism, as well.* Because egoism is the result of the animating appetite, it tends to be coherent; it attempts to surpass the *conventional integration* into society by *intrapsychic integrity.*

The coherent egoism, or the evolutionary and spiritualizing drive, prompts the intensely animate individual to seek the ultimate satisfaction in the surpassing of social conventions (which are utilitarian and organize the outer). Regardless of his participation in the effort of social organization, the individual can find integrity only through orientation toward the profound evolutionary meaning of life. The evolutionary intentionality of voluntary retention tends to a meaningful organization of the intrapsyche. The persistent disarrangement of this is the essential peril and the profound cause of social disorder. In the essentially animated individual, the meaning of life or the evolutionary growth is transformed into *essential desire*, into the desire to be fulfilled and to acquire authenticity. Evolutionary growth, the directive meaning of life, demands, at its zenith, the sublimation of the individual: the harmonious integration of differentiated desires. The retention of excitations, the suspension of the reaction that is now voluntary in humans, leads toward an evolutionary ideal.

The adaptation to the socialized milieu, just like the adaptation to a natural environment for the animal, is merely an outer sign of evolutionary accomplishment. Its essential condition is intrapsychic and has an individual reach. It is the search for essential satisfaction (the harmonious reunification of desires). All the complexities of human life and the theoretical misunderstandings regarding meaningful conduct are due to the fact that the search for satisfactions is, on one hand, no longer exclusively guided by instinctive sureness, and, on the other, insufficiently subjected to the control of the valuating spirit. The human psyche in search of its satisfaction is exposed to errors and anxietudes, the specific character of that is the result of the *differentiation of animal unconscious into psychic instances that become partly conscious and remain partly extraconscious.* The nature of human anxietude, a phenomenon of retention that is repressive in character, can be comprehended from a study of the biogenesis of extraconscious instances.

D. THE CONSCIOUS AND THE EXTRACONSCIOUS

Freud, who first introduced the study of the extraconscious to psychology, distinguishes from the conscious instance called the "ego" two extraconscious instances: the "id" and the "superego." The id is the *animal unconscious*, the instinctivity, where psyche and organism are still indistinctly entwined. The unconscious continues, at the human level, to regulate vegetative functions, which are no longer under the control of the conscious ego. The Freudian superego is an instance of control that is both higher and lower than the conscious. Higher, because it considers the sphere of ethical values; lower, because it rigidly and obsessively imposes conventional values through parental interdiction. In the Freudian concept, the values appear as the result of the decomposition of the Oedipus complex, and we know that this complex presents in a sexualized form the link of lovingness that ought to bind children to parents. According to Freud, the ideal tie of lovingness contains, since childhood, a factor of guilty impurity to which the interdictions of parents are directed, and from which the child, in the course of the ontogenesis, can only liberate himself through repression. The superego thus falsely defined would retain the parental interdictions in the form of a rigid ideal of conventional and pseudosublimative obedience.

The excessively rigid superego presents itself as a conflictual instance, the source of a constant friction between moralizing pseudosublimation and repression, hence its pathogenic power. The superego thus conceived is closer to an underego, for it is the cause of the morbid deformation of the ego; it is more subconscious than superconscious, as the superego is pathologically opposed to conscious control. The entire Freudian theory is not based on biogenesis, but only on pseudo-oedipal ontogenesis, as the pansexual hypothesis is arbitrarily based on the myth of Oedipus. In spite of this necessary objection, it remains that Freud opened the way to the analysis of the extraconscious and its symbolizing expressions: dreams, myths, and psychopathic symptoms. By so doing, Freud enriched human knowledge with an important discovery that goes far beyond that of his overly sexualized hypothetical structure. What he left to the effort of social sciences is neither more nor less than a new mode of thinking: the demand to psychologically rethink the illogical projections of desires and subconscious anxieties. He had the admirable lucidity to call his theory on instances a "rough hypothesis." He says on the subject: "It is a hypothesis as there are many in sciences. The first ones are very rough. One could say *open to revision*"[1] (Freud, 1950, p. 139). In light of the master's declaration, it seems difficult to grasp why his disciples endeavor to transform the "rough" hypothesis of the genesis of instances into an unattackable dogma. This error becomes easy to comprehend, however, when we admit that perhaps it could be one of the extraconscious illogisms, of which Freud noticed the obsessive aspect as well as the method of elucidation. Jung in particular among Freud's disciples contributed a considerable addition to the theory of extraconscious instances.

Jung discovered the superconscious instance by studying the mythical imaginations that are common to all peoples and by concluding that mythical images contain the guiding values or the orientation toward the evolutionary meaning of life in a symbolically veiled form. This research led him to oppose the Freudian superego, which is truly the subconscious, with a new instance, the "self." Jung (1938) defines the self as follows: "The unknown and much researched center of personality, the indefinable point where antinomies reconcile" (p. 228).

Perhaps, however, this instance is actually "definable." The function of the *superconscious*, its opposition to the *subconscious*, and its relation to the *conscious* are perfectly definable if we comprehend their biogenesis from the animal *unconscious* and its immanent finalism, which is the transformational dynamism of anxiety, the retentional energy or the driving force of psychic evolution.

*   *   *

Hominization is misunderstood if humans are viewed only as beings that became conscious; it should be understood that evolution toward the conscious necessarily implies the advent of extraconscious instances, one more-than-conscious, the other less-than-conscious. This most significant differentiation is implied in the very nature of the conscious instance, for it is at once half-imaginative and half-cognitive. Imagination, by being exalted, is degraded into subconsciousness; in order to remedy it efficiently, cognition necessarily implies the possibility of a superconscious control.

All the instances that are thus mutually conditioned and dynamically linked participate in the intimate valuative deliberation; the elements of the valuation are the motives of action, and its goal is the harmonizing reintegration of contradictory motives: freedom from the subconscious hold and its tendency to play with the imaginative presatisfactions to the extent of—involutionally—degrading them into a kind of falsely seductive and pathologically obsessive daydream. The superconscious, which emerges from instinctivity as well, but retains the positive quality of foresight evolved into clear-sighted intuition, opposes the fallacious promises of satisfaction of the subconscious.

Neither the superconscious nor the subconscious could influence the hesitant choice of the conscious if the possibilities of a disharmonizing perversion or harmonizing spiritualization were not foreshadowed by the faculty of imagination, which is halfway between the conscious and the extraconscious.

Imagination likes to combine and recombine the various images that represent promises or threats from the environmental reality. It incurs the risk of exalting desires and anxieties. Conversely, the cognitive intellect, a conscious faculty like imaginative foresight, in turn uses the images in order to get objectifying abstractions that are free from the affective hold, rather than semiconscious daydreams. The potentially generalizing abstractions that are fixed in linguistic concepts do not become stereotyped and sporadic signs—as are warning signs in the animal—but multiform, flexible, and variable, fit to logically formulate the modifications of the outer world where the desired or feared objects lie, according to their cause and effect.

The confrontation between the causal modifications of the outer world and the possibilities of motivating modification (whether sublime or perverse) of psychic interiority constitutes the "dialogue" between instances: the intimate deliberation that, unknown to oneself, occurs ceaselessly in the depths of the human psyche, as it is partially extraconscious.

The elucidation of the causal bonds, of the outside world, as well as the inner world (where causality is motivating), proves difficult and the faculty of objective representation is separated from subjective imagination only slowly throughout the evolutionary epochs that mark the history of the human species.

*   *   *

To employ a spatial image, we could say that the conscious is merely a minute emergence out of the immensity of the unconscious, in which humans remain immersed by their extraconscious instances, the residue of animal instinctivity. The unconscious continues to differentiate itself evolutionally. This differentiation is now operating under the influence of the conscious, which should be more and more able to penetrate the depths of the unconscious from whence it emerged. The conscious is nevertheless incapable of differentiating—elucidating— the immensity of the unconscious. It reaches only the "superficial zones."

The unconscious, even in its primitive form, remains an instance of the human psyche. It retains, for the greater part, its automatic and organic reactivity, but this latter relates only to the vegetative function, which is regulated by reflex reaction.

The two new instances of the *subconscious* and the *superconscious* originate from the interreactional dynamism between unconscious and half-conscious. They exist only in latent potentiality and only sound or unhealthy deliberation will activate the real functioning of the extraconscious instances from the preestablished latency.

The *subconscious* is the result of a morbid distortion of the primitive unconscious. Imagination, a half-conscious function and therefore half-unconscious as it is exalted to the detriment of cognitive representation, regresses toward the unconscious. The perversely blinded and exalted imagination loses its natural function of half-conscious future prospection without recovering the adaptively determining force of blind reflex. Henceforth involuntary, determination degrades into obsession.

Imaginative exaltation and its result of perverse blinding indicate a loss of prospective patience. Retentional energy loses patience. Instead of advancing toward a long-term attack on the difficulties (toward the active attainment of projects or toward a deep cogitation that is capable of elucidating them), the impatient affect is content with imaginative presatisfaction, immediately available, anytime.

Affectively exalted imagination is severed from the real discharge and uselessly seeks a way out by regressing to unconscious automatism and its primitive means of instant satisfaction: the reflex reaction. But the unconscious, invaded by an affectivity that is too exalted and too diversified in various desires and projects, is not fit to satisfy the imaginative demands. Its primitive function of automatic discharge is disturbed. The demand of discharge, which is now imaginatively exalted and really inhibited, is blocked; it is halfway between real activity and dream. Nothing happens but the inactive pseudo-satisfaction of reveries. *The indissoluble ambivalence of intentions determines the pathological character of subconscious reactions, the obsessive impatience and onirical explosion.*

Two characteristics of the subconscious are the lack of conscious adaptive qualities (choice and reflection) and the loss of unconscious adaptive qualities (the sureness of instinctive foresight and the security of automatic reactivity). The result is a disoriented maladjustment of the subconscious, the inexhaustible and uncontrollable source of growing and irritated insecurity. It constantly provokes anxious accidents, while it gradually becomes unable to overcome them. Always exacerbated by new insuperable accidents, the subconscious anxietude accumulates and stagnates. The various forms of accidental anxiety eventually congeal in a permanent state of morbid anxiety, the most characteristic trait of the subconscious.

In all points of view, the *superconscious* is diametrically opposed to the subconscious instance (except that both emerge from the primitive unconscious and are onirically expressed). The productions of the superconscious, at once sure and lucid, which are a blend of the elucidating function of the conscious and the instinctively sure function of the unconscious, do not, however, achieve the conceptual precision of intellectual thought. The superconscious instance is also expressed by figurative representation, like the subconscious, *but this form of imagination acquires a character of creative sublimeness.* In the higher interest of the individual (of the being that should remain undivided despite the diversification of desires), the superconscious intuitively creates the unifying visions of thought (truth), of sensitivity (beauty), and of activity (goodness).

These guiding images, the inspiration of sublimely intuitive imagination, are not causally linked like the concepts of the intellect, and their link is not associative and subjectively affective as in perverse imagination. The representative visions of the superconscious are established by analogies. Thus, they grasp the evolutionary meaning of life, because evolution itself proceeds by a hierarchic variation, each higher form of which remains essentially analogous to the lower forms in spite of the accidental diversification. As beings at the half-conscious stage, humans can, because of their sometimes hesitant, sometimes subconsciously obsessive choice, ruin the hierarchic unification that ties all their desires, and therefore all past life, to future life. However, the evolutionary law that, stage by stage, guided the species to the emergence of semiconscious life still demands unification. *The superconscious analogical visions (truth, beauty, goodness) present themselves as imperatives that have the same character of sureness as animal instinct,* although not as immediately determining because the capacity of conscious choice can either bow to the superconscious imperative or reject it.

*   *   *

However, rejection cannot happen without the manifestation of the most imperative form of anxiety, guilt.

The evolutionary imperative that is formulated by the symbolical onirism of mythical images has the characteristic of a guiding ideal. Creative imagination and its evolutionary imperative no longer operate a primitive (overall and automatic) unification, as does instinct, the guide of animal reactivity. It includes the totality of desires.

The guiding vision of the superconscious offers humans the reunification of the various desires, otherwise they would fall victim to the essential anxiety called guilt. *As unity in diversity is harmony, the superconscious imposes the harmonization of desires* that alone can overcome the disorientation of accidental anxieties and alone can generate the meaningful direction of activity on a higher plane.

The superconscious imperative, which is an evolved form of un-

conscious instinctivity, must, in order to deploy all its adaptive potential, evolve into a clear-sightedness that is no longer onirically veiled
but capable of conceptual formulation. *The conscious attempts to expand in the direction of the superconscious cannot happen without the
effort to elucidate the perverse functioning of the subconscious.* Sureness can be rediscovered only by an intrapsychic elaboration of this
ideationally and ideally representative certainty called truth. But as
long as the imperative of truth (which alone can determine the conscious adaptation to the evolutionary meaning of life) does not find a
precise scientific formulation, the guiding images of the superconscious will remain the unique ancestral way designed to oppose the
subconscious exaltation of desires and anxieties.

The human spirit, a seeker of truth, should not recoil from the
demand to understand the essential truth hidden in its own extraconscious productions, mythical dreams, nocturnal dreams, and psychopathic symptoms. Psychopathic symptoms, which are the symbolic
expression of repressed desires and anxieties, are the exact measure of
the aberration regarding the meaning of life.

Superconscious and subconscious confront each other in nocturnal dreams, where the vacillating conscious is excluded. Dreams continue the daytime deliberation that had been abandoned because it
was submerged by the fallacious overflow of semi-imaginative, subconscious reveries. In the symbology of their images, dreams propose an
essential and harmonizing solution to everyday problems that have
been in suspense. They indicate to the dreamer the false motives that
prevent him, in the waking state, from lucidly deliberating. Without
our knowing it, our waking state, rather than being lucid, is too often
merely an intrication of unfinished thoughts and onirical imaginations, an imbroglio of reveries provoked by dead-end ambitions, bitter-
ness and complaints, or the whole parade of ruminating resentments.

Myths, which are superconscious productions, represent the laws
of harmony and disharmony. Their underlying theme is no longer individual bewilderment, but the lawfulness that presides over the
meaningful or meaningless deliberation of each and every human
being. Intrapsychic conflicts are symbolically externalized: The mythical hero (symbol of humanity) fights demons (symbol of subconscious
temptations) and monsters (symbols of devouring passions) with the
help of divinities (symbol of the harmonizing forces of the superconscious).

*The extraconscious is thus composed of three elements: the primi-
tive unconscious, the morbid subconscious, and the intuitive supercon-*

scious. All forms of human anxiety and of the effort to surmount it are determined by the interplay (play and counterplay) of these elements.

Accidental anxiety (which relates to the influx of excitations) comes from the conflict between the two faculties of the conscious instance that are intended to elaborate the discharge: imagination and cognition.

Guilty anxiety, which is of an essential nature because it concerns the inadequate arrangement of retained excitations (essential weakness), is due to the inadequacy of conscious elucidation and thereby to a conflict waged between the superconscious and the subconscious.

It cannot be stated too strongly that the differentiation of the human psyche—the genesis of extraconscious elements that is necessarily complementary to the appearance of the half-conscious element —is a phenomenon of biopsychic evolution, an evolutionary product of the retentional energy seeking its discharge. *The intrapsyche as a whole is defined by anxiety and its sublime and perverse transformations.*

* * *

Because the problem of the genesis of the human psyche is fundamentally significant, it is not superfluous to consider it from a complementary perspective, even at the risk of repetition. We must insist upon a cardinal phenomenon: the expansion of the driving appetites and the consequent multiplicity of desires, whether spiritual, material, or sexual.

In humans, the inner self bears the whole world in the form of images that are apt to excite and overexcite the appetites, independently of the presence or lack of an actually perceived excitant in the environment. Because of this *self-excitation*, the psychic functioning is no longer immediately linked to the natural appetites of the soma or to the conditions of satisfactions presented by the environment. The psyche acquires a relative independence in relation to the soma and to the environment, which risks the provocation of an anxiety-laden rupture of the vital unity of psyche, soma, and environment, by an imaginative overexcitation. The loss of instinctively immediate contact with the somatic and environmental reality is the cause of human anxietude. In order to avoid becoming morbid, anxietude requires appeasement, which is impossible without an elucidating premeditation of the inner causes—the secret motives—of imaginative self-excitation. The unique, efficient palliative is, of course, cleansing *self-observation.*

The human psyche thus acquires a kind of independence in relation to the soma because desires multiply to the extent that they overstep the elementary need for self-preservation. The preconscious spirit becomes the self-organizer, which is autonomous and responsible for human anxietude in case of failure.[2]

*   *   *

Since the animal has only natural needs that, as they are common to the species, cannot be individually and imaginatively exalted, we can rightfully say that the bodily organization and the instinctive prescience of the environment are, in animals, the manifestation of an "organizer-spirit" that is inherent in the evolutionary growth, but still preconscious. With this understanding, we can correctly state that in spirit the animal innocently reposes in the meaning of life. The animal organism is perfectly adapted to the environment and has no possibility of aberration in relation to the evolutionary meaning.

Genetically understood, instinctive prescience performs two functions: *preserving adaptation to the environment* and *incorporation into the evolutionary meaning*. In spite of this perfect complementarity, adaptation in animals has, nonetheless, an imperfect aspect: The overall nature of instinctivity is unsuitable to ward off all perilous environmental modifications. Inadequate foresight can be aggravated in some circumstances to the extent that it becomes a life threat.

The evolutionary step of the blossoming of the conscious ineluctably results in the loss of the innocent repose in the meaning of life. The two evolutionary functions, which were perfectly united in the animal unconscious, are differentiated and can thereby oppose each other. One of these evolutionary functions, the *adaptation to the environment*, which is henceforth exerted by the conscious through its semilucid representation of the excitant world and its dangers, is still exposed to the subconscious confusion that caused the loss of innocence. The other unconscious function, the *adaptation to the evolutionary meaning*, is transformed into a more-than-conscious or superconscious prevision. It represents the demand of the evolutionary spirit to purify desires; only an individual effort of sublimation-spiritualization can accomplish this task. The elementary need to safeguard unity, which became a superconscious demand of harmonization, is opposed to the vital danger of dispersion by excessive multiplication of desires.

The conflictive situation of the human being acquires a scope that primarily concerns the intrapsychic relation between the superconscious and the subconscious rather than the immediate relation with the outside. The stake of this totally internalized struggle is no longer environmental adaptation, but reintegration into evolutionary meaning. From accidental, the conflict became essential. The anxiety accompanying the vicissitudes of this expanded and internalized conflict is no longer of an accidental nature, but of an essential scope. The essential danger or the loss of repose in spirit (the dynamic repose that is also called "impulse of evolutionary surpassing") cannot be achieved without the emergence of a superconscious warning that denounces the *peril that is no longer physical death but "death" of the spirit (the exaltation of desires)*. This warning regarding the vital fault manifests as a feeling of guilt. By this *essential anxiety* or guilt, the superconscious indicates the trespass of evolutionary law that demands integration in spite of the differentiation. At the same time, the superconscious inflicts a sanction upon the conscious instance in default, the torment of guilty anxiety. The superconscious thus accomplishes the function of a judging instance, *conscience*. It is essential to make a clear distinction between ethical conscience and the conscious or utilitary intellect.[3]

We would fail to recognize the relation of lawfulness that exists between the evolutionary functions of the conscious and the extraconscious if we were to introduce a supernatural determination. According to the secret intuition of the myth, the divinity-judge is a symbol of superconscious self-determination. The *committed sin*, the guilt, and *its sanction* or anxiety are linked in guilty anxiety. Biologically speaking, *the sanction is not overadded to the trespass. It is inherent to guilt: It is guilt itself.*

The biologically founded lawfulness concerns the energetic exchanges between the elements of the extraconscious. The subconscious tendency to justify falsely the unlimited multiplication of accidental desires opposes the superconscious impulse of reunification, an impulse we could call "essential desire." As the energetic tension is provided by the totality of desires in quest of a satisfying discharge, *the psychic energy is distributed between accidental desires and the essential desire*. The more intense the essential desire, the less captivating the temptation of exaltation of accidental desires. Conversely, the exaltation of accidental desires diminishes the unifying energy of the essential desire, which, as it gradually loses hope of attainment, is charged with anxiety of an essential scope.

The essential desire should unite all accidental desires in a rejoicing harmony; this attainment is the hope of life. The imaginative exaltation of accidental desires transforms hope into despair, the sound formation of the psyche into morbid distortion. *Insofar as the essential and superconsciously foreseeing desire becomes anxious, because of an exaltative failure of the half-conscious instance, its charge of essential anxiety concerns all exalted desires; and their nuance of guilt indicates the fault committed by the individual in relation to his own higher interest.* In the inner smearing that guilty anxiety creates, all exalted desires are grouped together as an undifferentiated magma and included in a single vague feeling of *self-judgment* and *self-condemnation.* In other words, the feeling of guilt is added to each accidental anxiety, which is due to the incapability of the half-conscious to mobilize meaningful means for a discharge that conforms to the demands of environmental reality.

Only once the stages of the biogenesis of the psyche and its final differentiation into contradictory instances are established is it possible to reassemble the details and to expand their interfunctional scope in order to constitute a dynamic view of the entire complex functioning of the human psyche. The product of retentional energy, the interplay of elements of the extraconscious determines the intimate and intrapsychic work, and it results in either morbid exaltation of anxiety or its spiritualization-sublimation, which is transformation into joy. Retention, which is exclusively evolutionary in the animal realm, becomes liable to be perverted in humans precisely because of the emergence of guilty anxiety and its possible subconscious repression. We must understand how *the repressive form of retention* produces involutionary states (mental illnesses) that are diametrically opposed to the evolutionary way, which brings the blossoming of always more lucid and clear-sighted functions.

NOTES

1. Italicized words here appear in English in Freud's text.

2. In the animal, the psyche is not yet clearly differentiated from somatic appetite (organic hunger). The wild animal, as it is continually exposed to life-threatening dangers, knows fear only in its instinctively profound form, which is immediately linked to the basic need for self-preservation. Higher animals, however, are deprived of neither imagination nor intelligence. Their imaginative fear potentially contains anxiety. In herbivores, for example, a rough form of imaginative fear, a sketch of anxiety, is added to the perceptive fear. Even if the aggressing animal is not present, herbivores are haunted by the possibility of

its sudden emergence, which is shown by the constant exploration of the visual and olfactory horizons. Moreover, higher animals can dream. We can suppose that their dreams contain as many olfactory images as visual, but present only isolated situations and dreaming images that do not tie into a story with an underlying meaning.

In the human psyche, the sequence of the imagery is manifest not only in the dream, but in the daydream. Vacillating between the exalted apprehension of desires or anxiety, it creates, in the case of frequent self-exaltation, a nervous irritability that can be exacerbated to delusion and hallucinations (where desired or anxiety-laden objectives are attained by pseudointerpretation or pseudoperception).

In this respect, it is instructive to observe that an analogous state of infuriated or fearful irritability can be provoked in the animal to which one alternately shows and refuses bait. The repetition of such experiences makes the animal mean and aggressive. However, it is quite erroneous to claim that this is a case of experimentally provoked neurosis or psychosis. The decisive difference lies precisely in the fact that the nervous irritation of the animal is not due to imaginative self-exaltation, but exclusively to the artificial frustration of its elementary driving appetite. This is to say that, as always, the analogical comparison becomes a cause of error by omission of the radical difference between the elementary drives of the animal and the expanded drives of humans.

3. As a consequence of the symbolizing onirism—a function that can be explained biologically—the superconscious personifies its own functioning and represents it as mythical images that remain essentially valid for each individual, provided they are understood as images. Their concretized figuration contains the biologically veracious meaning of the life and destiny of the human species, as a secret significance. The myths of all peoples symbolize the biological phenomenon of the advent of the conscious and the loss of innocence. This biological event of primary importance is symbolized, in the Judaic myth, by Adam (the figure of nascent humanity), who, because he ate the fruit of the tree of knowledge (the symbol of the advent of the conscious), is exiled from the animal paradise (the symbol of repose in spirit).

6

Anxiety and Its Extraconscious Transformation

Anxiety is produced by an imaginative retention of fear. Anxiety or fear imaginatively represented is a state of restlessness that is not roused from an actual peril, but from a danger that is only envisioned as possible. The event that triggers fear is always in the present; the threat that provokes anxiety lies in the past or in the future. (In certain cases—for instance, an outbreak of organic illness—there is an overlap of fear with anxiety because the constant, actual danger causes an anxiety-laden apprehension for the future.)

Fear disappears the moment its actual cause ceases to exist. Some restlessness may remain, because of its prolonged repercussion, but this state no longer possesses the primitive character of fear. What finds itself in contradiction with reality is no longer the sole and unique desire for security, but a chain of desires of all orders; exacerbated by the peril, imagination enters and starts to work more or less convulsively. *The play of imagination on fear is anxiety.* This leads to a new definition: Anxiety is the *contrast between imagination and reality.*

Imagination might foresee a truly existing threat and, in this case, anxietude is natural, accidental, and transitory. Anxiety in this form is a positively significant warning: it stimulates the mobilization of a meaningful effort that is able to expel the threat. But the anxiety-laden apprehension might foresee in the imagination dangers that are actually nonexistent, or it might exaggerate true threats. Imagination risks becoming unreal, morbid, and permanent.

Instead of using imaginative foresight to ward off threat, which is *the natural function of imagination*, morbid anxiety only manages to re-present (present again) the danger, and so prolongs the state of confusion (the loss of presence of mind) that is the most characteristic trait of sudden fear. *Morbidly anxious imagination is a relative of panic fear*; rather than stimulating defense reactions, it succeeds in inhibiting them and even in paralyzing them. Anxiety is exalted concerning what could have happened or what could happen if the danger were to reappear. Not fit to arm itself against eventualities, imagination in its pathogenic form, while it prolongs the state of confusion and panic or the absence of presence of mind, is content to turn around and about in the mind. It lingers and exaggerates distressing consequences.

Moreover, the imaginative play may attempt to ward off anxietude by minimizing the incurred and anticipated peril. The disorientation provoked by past danger is likely to seek solace in unreal parades filled with bravado. Insofar as imagination is exalted, there is great risk that all data regarding past events or future situations will be distorted; this would result in a progressive nonadaptation to reality and its dangers. Imagination exalts the anxiety-laden contrast with reality or eliminates it fallaciously without accomplishing the essential, real effort (which is only a counterform of exaltation); imagination, frightened by its own inventions or triumphant in illusory success, will result in falsely interpreting past danger, each present situation, and all future threats.

Finally, because anxiety is a phenomenon of imaginary representation, its time span is not limited by the disappearance of threats, as with fear. Anxiety can evoke the anxiety-laden object and situation anytime, delight at leisure in the illusion of victory, or be distressed by the pangs of defeat. As it constantly plays with gratuitous possibilities, imagination loses its faculty of prospection. It escapes into the impossible and becomes lost in the unreal. Because of the great facility of its gratuitous production and its power of disorientation, morbid anxiety can invade the psyche and assume an essential significance in psychic life.

Imagination in its natural and morbid forms must be distinguished from creative imagination, which is a superconscious function.

* * *

The objection that morbid anxiety is not produced exclusively by the individual and his imagination, but can be provoked by environmental reality as well, could be raised against these basic conclusions (which are inaccessible when viewed from the outside. According to the explanation of outside observation, the frequent repetition of real dangers would provoke a series of fear crises that immerse the psyche into a quasi-constant state of anxiety. Is it not the most widespread opinion that the frequency of upsets, troubles, and setbacks produce the anxious state, or nervousness? The problem of intrapsychic anxietude and its morbid aggravation prompts the search for the motives of this justifying tendency that denies intimate cause, the subject's own fault, to admit only environmental and potentially traumatizing causes. *Anxiousness* is, indeed, a special case of intimate anxietude. It is due to the memory of past failures or inhibiting memories that tend to frighten the subject to the extent that all future obstacles are immediately pictured as insurmountable.

For repeated failures to link themselves successfully into a chain that leads to a state of anxiousness, isn't it necessary that, in the periods exempt of danger, the individual evoked past fear and represented the danger to himself by way of affective imagination? Therefore, the cause of anxiety, even in such a case, is more in the individual than in the reality that surrounds him. Indeed, the environmental reality plays an extremely important role in the production of anxiety, as it provides imagination with the opportunity for exaltation. Opportunities, nevertheless, are only codetermining. The true determination is intrapsychic; it resides in the positive or negative response, whether vitally meaningful or meaningless, of the individual. *The essential is not what happens to the individual, but the—individually characteristic—way in which he reacts and motivates his reactions.*

The psyche also possesses a positive form of reactivity, even toward repeated dangers. If, in times exempt of danger, the individual, instead of giving himself up to exalting imagination, were to look for a confrontation with reality and its demands—if he knew how to avoid the essential fault of prolonging the loss of presence of mind in the imagination—he would successfully evoke future danger without imagining, through exaltation, easy victory or total defeat. The reference to reality, whether environmental or intrinsic, will allow him to understand what needs to be done to truly overcome in the event danger were to reappear. The subject thus rediscovers an attitude of courageous and meaningful attack, instead of imaginative escape and the resulting morbid anxiety. Past fears that have been truly overcome no longer weld into anxiousness; it follows that anxiety of dangers to come diminishes and can even disappear. The difficulties of life are no longer viewed as insurmountable dangers.

Nonetheless, if explaining these two opposed reactions seems

simple, nothing is actually more difficult than to avoid the one and imperturbably attain the other. All of us have too often failed in the effort
to maintain the meaningful reaction, not to be tempted to feel some
mistrust regarding its efficiency. And, nevertheless, would that doubt
itself not originate in an ever anxious representation of life (and especially of intimate life) and its difficulties? What could be worse than to
attribute to mistrust in ourselves the value of an objective argument
and to depreciate the sole salutary reaction in order to justify surrender? To defend the easy reaction of surrender falsifies the problem
—vitally the most important—and causes, by blinding imagination,
failure to recognize its intrapsychic process and the means to overcome
it.

Morbid anxiety is produced by the imagination that is insufficiently transformed into cognitive prospection, and this is where its
disastrous character of exalted contrast with reality comes from. This
contrast extends to the outer conditioning, to the excitant environment, also and foremost to the inner reality, to the intrapsychic causation or the elaboration of motives of future reactions. The motives of
deficient reactions, because they are anxiety-laden and provoke anxiety—they are painful to admit—tend to escape the conscious. The effort to understand—especially motives—remains almost always imaginatively distorted and degrades into *affective thought*. Thus exalted
imagination remains a series of desires and anxieties that *disguise
themselves as reflection* by the use of *an affectively fallacious argumentation* for justification.

Affective thought is the most familiar way of pseudocognitive
prospection. It is particularly blind to what it does not like to understand, and to the unavowed motives that underlie the imaginative interplay with desires. These motives become obsessive because they are
content with imaginative presatisfactions, and exalt them freely, leading them to chimerical combinations that seem to be of infinite wealth
and that, in truth, are but an impoverishment of *the sole raison d'être
of the desire: its potential of realization.* On the intrapsychic level of motivation, this impoverishment of the impulse of attainment causes a
ceaseless aggravation of the contrast with reality.

In order to understand anxiety in all its forms (whether natural,
morbid, accidental or essential), we must gain a better grasp of the nature of the imaginative play by becoming attentive to the means that
imagination has at its disposal to construct from desires the multitude
of its combinations.

* * *

Desire, the tension of the subject toward the object of his choice, is composed of two factors.

The first, objectal in nature, is the figurative representation of the coveted object; the other factor, subjective in nature, is the attraction exerted by the object toward the subject—*the promise of satisfaction*. The objectal factor is at the origin of cognition; the subjective factor leads to imaginary presatisfaction.

Cognition attempts to transform—as mentioned earlier—the objectal image into an abstract and objective concept. However, the abstractive elimination of affectivity is a theoretical process of logical formalism. In reality, thought remains more or less affectively tied to concrete objects.

The impatience of affect is nevertheless diminished as the conceptualization gradually succeeds in transforming the promise of a more or less imprecise satisfaction into *a represented goal*. The subject acquires the capacity to choose deliberately the means of realization of the desire, even if only on a long-term basis, or, possibly, to renounce the realization freely. *The more objective and conceptualized the objectal factor, the less obsessive the subjectivity of the affective factor.*

The complication created by the multitude of desires and their unlimited possibility of meaningless multiplication is the essential fact. However much the utilitarian calculus of the intellect strives to discipline desire, it will always be swamped by a multitude of other desires, the affective impatience of which demands immediate satisfaction to the detriment of reflection. That is why the processes of the imagination, which are very different from those of the intellect, have a predominant significance in practical life. Imagination links the affective factors of multiple desires into presatisfying games. It is most radically opposed to the conceptualization of the objectal factor of desires, for it needs the still nonobjective factors to create the unfolding of a seductive imagery, the subject of which is the subjugated spectator.

Nevertheless, imagination in its natural and prospective form is not in contradiction to the cognitive prospection; rather, it attempts to help it. Its groping games are seeking a preorientation as well as a presatisfaction. The attempt at orientation would be inefficient if prospective imagination (a relative, by its groping, of the primitive method of trial and error) did not dispose, on the one hand, of all promises of satisfaction, and, on the other, of all cognitive factors (which more or less faithfully represent the image of desired objects and of the obstacles to be overcome in their obtainment). By approximately taking into account environmental variations, prospective imagination becomes suitable to preadapt—somehow or other—by its various games, the promises of satisfaction (the subjective factor of desires) to the environmental conditions (objectal factor). In order to have a prospective value, *these linking games must be preceded by a work of dissociation that is exerted on the two factors that compose each desire.*

Thanks to this preliminary work, prospective imagination becomes fit to link and recombine, at leisure, the multitude of affective and cognitive factors that have been previously sorted. It selectively obtains, from originally retained desires, new desires that are less affectively impatient and are provided with a clear objectal representation. The condition is, however, that dissociations and recombinations are guided by the right superconscious valuation. New desires, because they are soundly valuated in accord with their promises of satisfaction, will tend to fix and to become preferential and habitual. They acquire the scope of *guiding motives* with a precise and constant determining power. Fixation into motives won't occur, however, without a repeated reminder of their "raison d'être." The wisdom of language clearly expresses this genetic relation between desire and motive. The motives are our "reason to act." Sound motives are the essentially reasoned, reasonable determining factors that are harmonizable because they are free of exaltation. By deliberately varying the motivating constellation of the deep energetic tension, imaginative preorientation successfully favors the cleansing of the psychic functioning.

The danger of perversion still persists. It occurs when the imagination forgets its function of preorientation and, because it is now morbid, thinks only of combining and recombining desires with the aim to fulfill illusory satisfactions that lack reference to the real and the realizable. Since it believes itself to be free from any restrictive limitation, imagination misuses its fallacious and vain omnipotence. Taking its confusing reveries for lucidly valuating reflections, imagination profusely creates new desires as numerous as they are exalted in impatient affectivity. The oblivion of the real as well as the reasonable can occur only in the grip of wrong subconscious valuations that are obsessively repeated, and that degrade sane motives into perverse, contradictory, and discordant motives.

There exists, between the effort of right valuation of desires and the weakness of wrong valuation, between motives that are right or wrong depending upon their value of satisfaction, a fluctuating relation that can, any time and under the influence of any deceitful imagination, degrade sane motives into morbid motives. Linguistic custom expresses the ceaseless fluctuation between perverting reveries and elucidating reasoning by the almost synonymous meaning of the phrases "I think," "I believe," "I estimate," "I imagine," "I ponder."

In our intimate deliberations, the deviation of logical thought into reveries is a frequent and unnoticed phenomenon. Through false self-justification we take the wrong for the right, the right for the wrong, the true for the false, the false for the true. The supposedly voluntary decisions are made from falsely justified reveries. Does it not follow that the elimination of false justifications could retransform perverse reveries into lucid thought and wrong motives into right motives? The escape into pseudosatisfying reveries is doubtlessly infinitely easier than a lucid attack on the tendency toward false, egocentric, and vain justification.

The common cause of all *illnesses of the spirit* is the falsely justifying *vanity* (*vanitas*: the void, the empty; devoid of meaning, devoid of value). Vanity is the cause of all mental illnesses because it is an escape from spiritualizing attack.

* * *

The problem of psychic functioning, in its sane and unhealthy, meaningful and meaningless, vitally satisfying and dissatisfying forms, is condensed in two biologically based attitudes, attack and flight. These two attitudes—one evolutionary, the other involutionary—have until now been described as intrapsychic functions, spiritualizing work, and imaginative games.

Since a genuine psychological comprehension demands a biological subfoundation, it remains to be demonstrated in detail that spiritualization and imaginative perversion result from a complication of the elementary biological phenomenon of the retention of excitations, or the transitory suspension of action.

Spiritualization, in a biological sense, is a retentional force. It takes on the problem of intrapsychic excitations and retained desires. The spiritualizing attack prepares the propitious moment and the meaningful direction for their discharge. Vain reveries are a retentional weakness, a forced and convulsing retention that results in blocking the active discharge. Egocentric escape into the mental convulsions of imaginative exaltation becomes the cause of this other weakness of retention, which is banalizing deconvulsion. Banalization, an eruptive discharge of egocentric desires deprived of all retentional force, is, like the mental convulsion of nervosity, an escape from the demand of a preliminary work to arrange retained desires. But, unlike nervosity, banalization does not flee in reveries, it is a hastened escapism toward active discharge.

A. IMAGINATIVE ESCAPE

In fleeing the intrapsychic work of ordering constructively, exalted imagination attaches affective energy to the representation of objectives that are inaccessible in the present situation and most likely always beyond reach. This appears as omnipotence and increased freedom of choice, but it is, rather, a regression to stereotyped monotony. Reveries tirelessly ruminate over vague, unfinished projects (material worries, sexual daydreams, pseudospiritual ambitions and aspirations).

These promises of unlimited satisfactions lead up to flight into the absolute. They create absolutely unattainable *exalted tasks*. Ineluctable disappointments provoke a desperate flight sometimes into past regrets and sometimes into an anxiety-laden apprehension of the future. The refusal to admit the committed faults—the repression of errors and faults—provokes flight into the subconscious pseudorefuge, where the fugitive meets the most serious of all dangers. His imaginative self-dissatisfaction turns against him. It turns into essential self-dissatisfaction, into useless remorse and guilty torments. The more and more anxious flight searches for an outlet in the most illusory defense, and the self-pursuit of the culprit is transformed into indictment of the world. The false, vain self-justification creates a pseudoreality. The affected subject soon will corrupt his relationship with the environment and with others. Locked in his chimerical world, he becomes eventually unable even to judge himself. As he becomes a phantasm in his own eyes, he knows only how he valuates himself in comparison to others—sometimes higher and sometimes lower—so that to the anxiety of facing outer obstacles is added *the even more poignant anxiety concerning the opinion of others*. Hypersensitive on one hand, and, on the other, surrounded by a world of which he ceaselessly professes the injustice, the subject falls into sentimental self-pity for all his setbacks, which, most of the time, he insidiously provokes. All these unavowed confusions, a cause-effect of growing anxiety, ceaselessly reinforce his tendency to flee from a reality that he considers hostile and dangerous.

Thus, to flee into imaginative fantasy can be accomplished by two stereotyped paths. The first, the *escape* outside environmental reality, seduces by the vain hope of a material, sexual, and pseudospiritual order; the other, *the vain justification of one's own deficiencies* along with an *indicting projection of others*. This confusion leads more and more to the misunderstanding of intrapsychic reality, the truth about oneself.

* * *

Imagination of escape and imagination of justification reduce the spiritualizing courage to a self-complacent pathos. Escape into daydreams, which has become pathological and complaining, is characterized by the loss of conscious presence of mind, just like any dream. Like in dreams, in *reveries with open eyes*, one is at rest in relation to the real world and its difficulties. However, the difference is the rest in nocturnal sleep is natural and transitory.

In the daydream state, on the other hand, the mobility operates and the will elaborates, in the grip of overflowing affectivity, incoherent decisions that translate into conflicting and maladjusted actions. From lethargy the will is reduced to impulsiveness; reflection becomes atrophied. Reactivity regresses—in the form of obsession—into automatism and reflex. This morbid regression into undifferentiated reactivity causes the subject to need all his diminished energy to defend his chimerical world against the threat of seeing it collapse at each confrontation with real facts.

Action, when it becomes indispensable, is exerted at countercurrent. Deprived of any effort of adaptation, it obsessively repeats the same attack and defense attitudes suggested by hypnotizing anxiety (mistrust, resentment, sulking, vexation, need to win, and so on). In the advanced stages, imaginative self-suggestion is brought down into self-hypnosis. The flight into stereotyped resentments—flight intended to avoid the complications of a lucid clarification—produces stereotyped activity and also illogical actions of onirical expression. The irritability of the nervousness grows worse. It eventually produces neurotic symptoms, obsessions and phobias that express repressed, symbolically disguised desires or anxieties.

Obsessional neurosis is distinguished from imaginative reveries by the fact that the onirism of the desires of attack and flight are actively discharged, but only under symbolic disguises that are anxious precautions with a phobic characteristic. Phobic anxiety is no longer only an intimate feeling. It is openly manifest in gestures—illogical acts or nervous twitching—that substitute for meaningful activity.[1]

* * *

The escape into imaginary satisfactions, the imaginative flight to escape reality, always brings more morbid states of anxiety and more real states of inhibition. The entire world and the most natural satisfactions can be eventually prohibited. The first agreeable and seductive imaginative game gradually leads to a more and more unbearable disorientation that is imbricated with complications and heavy with torments. Morbid states result that range from nervosity to neurosis and psychosis.

It is very important to understand the energetic economy—or, rather, the lack of economy—that is at the foundation of the reversal of imaginative pleasure into torment of disorientation. The negative energy or the anxiety-laden affectivity that invades the disoriented subject or the nervous patient is composed of residues of all the inadequately discharged past excitations. The anticipated future is darkened with anxiousness that is a feeling issued from past setbacks and that determines in advance the inadequacy of future reaction. The subject never lives in the present moment, in reality, but by preference in a time that no longer exists or doesn't exist yet, in an imaginary time, and therefore he never disposes of all his energy. The energy is not only dispersed in a multitude of falsely combined and recombined desires, but it also wears down when residues of past excitations or the free evocation of excitations to come are ceaselessly revolving in the mind. Each new excitation, because of this futile work, increases the chaotic congestion of exasperated desires. Mistrust of the chances of satisfaction offered by reality (which actually is to mistrust oneself—another word for guilt) can range from nascent doubt to certainty of the impossibility of any satisfaction, the mortal anxiety of despair. The accumulation of anxiety provokes attempts at imaginative exoneration. The release thus sought can be found only in an unreal and imaginative discharge, the indictment of others, of world, of life.

The nervous tension of now negative desires and their convulsed energy constitutes a psychic overburden that demands discharge. Not able to become productive, convulsed energy mobilizes its destructive force. *Anxiety becomes aggressive;* its various forms of expression are accentuated; accusation becomes anger, mistrust is aggravated into hate, and so on. The congestion finds expression in a state of overexcitation in a constant irritability that determines the incontinence of the affectivity. Overexcited affect explodes. *Imaginative flight is retransformed into disoriented attack.*

This reactive explosion of accumulated affect, this eruption of retroverted desires into aggressive anxiety, is, in fact, unsuitable to

modify the adverse conditions of the environment in a meaningful way.
It exerts only a provocative effect.

Others, attacked by these indictive accusations (imaginatively
prepared for some time) respond with explosions of their own aggressive anxiety according to their own distortion. The angry and hateful
accusation becomes reciprocal; mistrust is generalized. It is aggravated into the need each one has to triumph over others, which
provokes not only verbal aggression—slander and calumny—but active intrigue or an atmosphere of intrigue where triumph is assured by
unscrupulous attack. The psychic abscess created by the inflammatory
imagination bursts and infects everyone. The mutual aggression becomes a generalized behavior from accumulated false justifications.

In order to have a chance of success, the projects of triumph and
revenge are organized into banal, astutely meditated intrigue. Of all
individuals, the nervous person is the least able to use such strata-
gems. The excess of irritability blinds him and renders him incapable
of shrewd foresight. His guilty anxiety, which seeks a vain justification,
overloads him with ceaselessly manifested subtle scruples that, in
comparison with the lack of scruples of the others, becomes in his eyes
proof of his sublimeness. Instead of defending himself, the nervous person rather pities himself; he enjoys the pose of declamatory indignation that disarms him and predestines him to failure, a source of
increased anxiety. A pitiful victim in a hostile world, who is mean because of powerless rage yet assumes a pose of goodness, the nervous
has the tendency to transform his aggressivity into a cunning in-
tolerance, into a critic for improvement, the ceaseless sugary, ironic, or
fanatic (even often mute) insinuations of which possess a provocative
power almost greater than a transitory explosion of anger. Without his
knowing it, the neurotic ceaselessly provokes and mistreats the environment, which in fact gradually becomes, through the externalizations of his aggressive anxiety, the hostile world that existed only in
his interpretative imagination in the beginning of the process of distortion.

*   *   *

However, the cunning or angry externalizations of anxiety, which are
ill-fated by the effects they produce upon the social environment, do
not even liberate the intrapsyche. Only the extra-anxiety is evacuated;
a stagnant bottom remains that is constantly fed by failures and
rumination on disappointments. The relief thus obtained is only transitory, and the convulsive discharges of anger, like the venomousness

of repressed rages, leave the psyche in a state of exhaustion.

The disintegration of the force of resistance thus corresponds to the *increase of provocative incontinence*. The assault of the environment never ceases to increase, and the anxious subject, at once provocative and about to become a victim of this intrigue, endlessly disarms himself. The result is the unbearable amplification of the painful contrast between imagination and reality, the original cause of the state. With the aggravation of its cause, the morbid state is aggravated. The overexcited imagination panics. Its ultimate means of defense is to flee into madness. Anxiety about both environmental reality and truth about oneself produces the paroxysmal illness of the spirit: psychosis. The imagination of flight hallucinates a pseudoreality, while the imagination of justification becomes delirious.

The genesis of these states of progressive panic becomes understandable when we examine their analogical link with the *reaction of fright* as it is produced in animals at the paroxysm of fear. At the primitive level of fear, we saw that fright is produced when the attack is extremely perilous and escape is impossible. Rather than a reactive discharge by external movement, an emotional overload is produced that is an inner ambivalence between the opposing impulses of attack and escape, which creates panic and is unsuccessfully externalized.

In humans, the panic frenzy of psychosis is due to the same conflict of ambivalence. The difference, however, is that it no longer paralyzes the attack-escape instinctivity, but the imagination of evasion and aggression that is exalted to its paroxysm. The escape into complacent reveries becomes impossible due to the fact that reveries are reversed into a guilty anxiety that is gradually more haunting and unbearable. The attack that is directed against the world, the excessive indictment of others, becomes impossible because the explosions of powerless rage provoke counterattacks from the environment that are more and more dangerous and crushing.

Since anxiety is not only a psychic state but reaches more deeply into the whole organism, its progression toward different degrees of panic doesn't depend exclusively upon the morbid constellation of the psyche (the deregulated function of a provoked provoker) but includes also the somatic base and the hereditary constitution.

B. LUCID ATTACK AND MORBID ANXIETUDE

The two means of lucid attack are intellectual foresight and clear-sightedness of the spirit. The intellect attacks environmental obsta-

cles. Its foresight is utilitarian and conservative; it attempts to ensure
material security, the indispensable base of existence. However, use-
fulness is not necessarily meaningful. The scale of values—the degrees
of satisfaction—goes beyond environmental adaptation. As it envisions
only external success, the utilitarianism of the intellect is a calculus
for a close-reaching satisfaction. It thus remains exposed to the danger
of flight into imaginative exaltation, the attempt at a false ideal that
is attained insofar as the intellect is exalted to the extent that it
believes external success to be the ultimate meaning of life. Vainly exalted, the intellect becomes banalized. It feels authorized to seek material and sexual pleasures at any price, whether by ruse or by
violence.

The escape into banalization, which is pseudo-intellectually justified, can be controlled only by the higher force of the clear-sighted
spirit, which can foresee the disastrous results of the fallacious courage
of unscrupulous attack. The function of the spirit is to oppose the intellectual overvaluation of external success and to make inner success,
the harmonization of desires, take precedence. Only spiritualizing attack has the power to overcome the individual anxietude of neurosis
and the collective anxietude due to banalization.

Neurosis and banalization are intimately linked by their secret
motivation. Neurosis is the consequence of exalted indignation in the
face of the iniquity of a banalized world. Each man bears in himself, in
various degrees of intensity, banal temptation and ruminative indignation as well, which are the causes of neurotic irritability.

*   *   *

The anxiety-laden contrast between imagination and reality is the
evolved consequence of the fundamental discord "subject-object," and
"spirit-matter." At the human level, the discord can find an evolutionary transformation into harmonious concord, through spiritualization-sublimation. The appeasement can be obtained in one of two
ways: either by an active modification of reality to make it conformable
to meaningful desires (project of the nonperverted utilitarian intellect)
or by a sublimative modification that determines that the imagination
accepts the conditions of reality as interchangeable.

To be strong rather than weak, the *acceptation* opposes resigned
submissiveness and the powerless rage of indignation as well. In a
state of at once submissive and revolted resignation, the anxiety-laden
contrast is far from being abolished and exists in the ruminative form
of regrets and resentments.

Acceptance is a spiritually lucid and sublimative fighting force. Through it, self-mastery as well as mastery of the environment are performed at the highest degree of intensity. The man who can always change the changeable and accept the unchangeable will know how to fight and overcome any source of dissatisfaction.

The most highly evolved force of retention or acceptance proceeds by elimination of accidentally unattainable desires, but also—and especially—by the dissolution of inharmonizable desires, even in the case where they are attainable—despite their exaltation—by banal unscrupulousness. *Acceptance recovers the energy of dissolved desires and orients it toward meaningful attainments.*

Because of all these distinctive traits, acceptance is contrary to the convulsive oblivion of desire, an oblivion that is obsessive repression. Acceptance, which is opposed to obsession, is intimately tied to the process of spiritualizing elucidation. It is, in fact, its essential condition.

Indeed, acceptance demands clarification of the goal of desires, for only a clear and unquestionable knowledge of the impossibility of realization or of prejudices caused by meaningless realization enables the psyche to renounce them without regret. However, since intrapsychic reactions complete each other by reciprocity, acceptance creates in turn the most favorable condition for spiritualizing elucidation. As it presents the highest degree of retention, acceptance exposes desires to the intrapsychic work of elucidating valuation for as long as possible. It collaborates thus in order to clarify promises of satisfaction.

There is no spiritualization without acceptance, or acceptance without spiritualization. Because of the sublimation of affective components and the spiritualization of representative factors, desires that are free from imaginative exaltation can be harmonized. Because of the spiritualization-sublimation, psychic energy is oriented toward the ideal meaning life: *the mastery of excitations.*

The spiritualization-sublimation, the positive result of intrapsychic work, transforms desires into meaningful motives. It accumulates energy in the form of *true ideas and just ideals.* The objectified energy which is condensed into guiding values acquires the potential of an active discharge that can influence the social environment in a meaningful way. The influence is not only of a civilizing order, like intellectual work. The spiritual discharge is *a creator of cultural values.*

The psyche can be compared to an accumulator-transformer that is intended to elaborate a provision of spiritual and sublimate energy that is transmittable and usable for any constructive aim, from the raw

energy of inflowing excitations. This positive transmission is uninter-
ruptedly accomplished throughout generations in spite of the defective
functioning of individual psyches.

The past cultural experience is condensed into ideas and ideals.
Individuals, according to their fecundity, find, as a base to their own
development, the truths created by the spiritualized desires and the
surmounted suffering of past generations.

But truth will always be more or less distorted by errors, which
are condensed into false ideologies. The spiritual attack, nevertheless,
will successfully overcome errors, because the evolutionary dynamism
of this cleansing process is not fed solely by good intentions (which are
too often only imaginative exaltations), but primarily by the representation of suffering, by anxiety that is the consequence of the error
and that demands to be evolutionally overcome.

The process of spiritualization, which generates sublimely transmittable energy, attempts to create, instead of a vicious circle, a stream
of ideas, a spiritual circuit that transmits the demand for clarification
of valid means of satisfaction from generation to generation. Gradual
clarification engages generations to incorporate into a common evolutionary effort.

*   *   *

The psychogenesis is accomplished from the most primitive retentional reaction to the highest manifestation of the voluntary retention of
the human being; it is gradually more intensely experienced. The evolution of the psychosomatic organism is only a special case of the evolutionary principle in which all that exists is included, from the atom
to the universe. This general principle that comprises life and prelife
is the demand for organization, that is to say, for harmony. Disorganization is the principle of disappearance, which, at the level of life,
is death. The retention is a disturbance of the harmony between the
living organism and its environment. It demands the reestablishment
of harmony, even if by the disappearance of the species and the appearance of a more highly organized species. Higher organization reestablishes the condition of existence, the harmony of energetic exchange
between object and subject and the influx of excitations and their discharge. Already at the most primitive level, the energetic exchange is
the means to "conciliate" the bipolar opposition of psyche/world, the
source of vital restlessness.

At the human level, the escape into exaltative imagination aggra-
vates the opposition between psyche and environment and transforms

vital anxiety into morbid anxiety. The spiritual attack, on the other hand, attains reconciliation with reality in its most sublime form; it creates the satisfying union of thought and reality, *the understood reality* or *truth*. The demand for understanding concerns not only the outer world, but also its complementary pole, the inner world and its sane or morbid functioning.

The harmony of the energetic exchange depends not only upon favorable conditions of the environment, but also, and primarily, upon the sane functioning of the human psyche, which is in charge of controlling the active response to excitations.

Unlike all other organisms that exist in a prevital or vital form, only the thinking being, the human, can live in a state of intimate disharmony. But he lives unhealthily. The disharmony of his thought determines mental illness.

The principal condition of vital satisfaction is *psychic health, which is defined by the capacity to discharge desires in a meaningful way, either outwardly or inwardly, by spiritualizing-sublimation—the opposite of repression—a process of preliminary discharge that prepares active discharge in its most meaningful form. Psychic insanity is defined as imaginative disturbance of the equilibrium or as an exaltation-inhibition of the reactive discharge (neurosis) or also, conversely, by the discharge without preliminary retention that is banalization.*

Understood in this manner, the whole of psychic functioning is determined, determinable and definable, because it is biologically founded. Yet biogenetic determinism does not abolish the possibility of individual freedom. The liberating effort consists of making the characteristic motivating determinations conscious, so deliberation can combine them sanely and at leisure; this is impossible without the effort of elucidating introspection. Each individual decision is in this way freely wanted, although determined by evolutionary history that leads from reflex to deliberating reflection. Nothing—except subconscious obsession—can prevent the thinking being from freeing himself of all anxiety-laden constraints, provided he brings his own motivating intentions into harmonious agreement with the mysterious organizing intentionality of nature. The freedom of will does not consist of doing everything one wants to do, but of ceasing to want the impossible, which is to oppose *with impunity* evolutionary finalism. *The opposite of freedom is not determination, for it can become evolutionary, or harmonizing, self-determination.* The opposite of freedom is subconscious obsession.

The incapacity for self-harmonization is a vital weakness, a vital guilt that manifests in the constraining anxiety of self-indictment: the feeling of guilt.

NOTES

1. The relationship between onirical obsession and dream becomes obvious in the common process of a symbolic shift of covetousness or guilty anxiety. In order to camouflage its powerlessness to attain the coveted objective, the affective tension of anxiety-laden desire ties itself to a substitute goal that only triggers the pretense of an action; the stereotypy becomes more complex and undertakes a whole set of illogical ceremonies. Thus in phobic obsessions, for instance, the guilty anxiety that underlies a desire that is felt to be impure is detached from the object that is obsessively coveted through imaginative exaltation. In order to authorize the attainment of a desire, the guilty interdiction shifts onto other objects or group of objects, which, henceforth, are considered untouchable. Any object can acquire, by way of association, this substitutive significance and the environment is hence populated by repulsive objects (a process also observable in the taboos of primitive peoples). The ceremonial precaution symbolically expresses anxiety in the real world (the threats and seductions of the real world are dangerously exalted and imaginatively multiplied as a result of the flight into the unreal world of chimera). In addition, phobia expresses the need for self-justification. This justifying meaning of the phobic taboo shelters a complex motivation that is composed of imaginative indictments of a world, the contact of which provokes corruption, and of sentimental complaints about living in a repulsive world; but it also betrays the vain aspiration to perfect purity and the attempt to justify oneself by the avoidance of impure contact. All these illogical precautions aim at preventing, if not the satisfaction of the original temptation, at least the rush of guilty anxiety that is tied to it. Anxiety no longer manifests at the moment of the attainment of the desire that is considered impure, but at the moment of the contact with the substituting object or objects, an "offense" that is more easily avoidable. However, since phobic anxiety alienates an amount of energy that is removed from the tension of impure desire, this latter might be attained only in an inhibited way, finding a part of its dynamism shorn.

7

Guilty Anxiety and Ethical Liberation

All psychic instances participate in intimate deliberation, in the effort of liberation or in its guilty failure. The destiny of humankind depends on the attitude toward guilty anxiety. *It is the pivot of intimate determination*, the link of the functioning of instances. It is the "message" sent to the conscious by the superconscious, and too often sabotaged by the subconscious.

Self-dissatisfaction—guilty anxiety—could not alert the conscious (even if only in the form of a vague feeling), *if humans did not have some foreknowledge of what they should do for their vital satisfaction.* Guilt, the feeling of aberration in relation to evolutionary meaning, demands as a principle of its existence a form of preknowledge of the evolutionary aim. Unlike animal instinctivity, which is organically and automatically determining, superconscious foresight, in order to have a determining influence, must act upon one of the two faculties of the half-conscious (reflection and imagination) that are at the source of the hesitant choice. Humans would be inept at living if they were guided only by the hesitancy of choice of the conscious.

The superconscious imperative is such that humans, like animals, remain subjects of the species and are guided, despite their own individuation, by a common instinctive foresight. The difference exists, nevertheless, that this instinctive link, which is now superconsciousness, no longer concerns solely somatic needs (nutrition and sexuality). Consequently, as drives expanded into a multitude of desires, so human superconsciousness has expanded. It became the guiding spirit and it individually dictates to each human the common law of harmonization that presides over the fate of the species, the ethical law

135

that implies individual sanction for each aberration or the feeling of
guilt and the pathogenic result of its repression. A biogenetic product,
the guilty anxiety of superconsciousness is a special case of the transformational dynamism of anxiety, the driving force of evolution that
determines everything that exists, including humankind, despite its
privilege of self-determination, which is prone to error. Because of this
proneness, the rectifying warning exists not only in the form of individual guilt, which is immediately attached to each error; the superconscious prevision—veracious because instinctive, and onirical
because extraconscious—has been ancestrally condensed into the
guiding images of mythical symbolism.

The evolutionary goal of mythical prescience is to oppose the
disharmonizing intention of perverse imagination with its warning-
veto: the guilty anxiety that is an individual and evolutionary stimulus
to the effort of reharmonization.

The originally mythical guilt generates an intrapsychic discord
which is unbearable on a long-term basis and thus determines the effort of reconciliation with oneself. However, as the onirical intention of
mythical superconsciousness is not constitutive (as is animal instinctivity) but only an indication of direction, the conscious choice, instead
of responding with a liberating avowal of the superconsciously revealed fault, may attempt to reestablish the intrapsychic concord between instances in a fallacious manner by repressing the warning of
guilty anxiety with a false, vain self-justification.

Diametrically opposed to liberating determination of the superconscious, repression creates the obsessing determinism of the subconscious, the final product of which is the caricatural counterform of
mythical onirism, the psychopathic symptom.[1]

Subconscious determinism not only generates onirical symptoms. Because of its obsessing irreducibility, it also generates stereo-
types pertaining to character, along with the parade of erroneous
ideologies, illogical prejudices, conformist precautions that have been
erected as principles, dogmatic solace, fanatical bias, and the like.

If, on the other hand, the psychic constellation answers the superconscious determination through an understanding avowal rather
than negatively (by denying the revealed fault), an effort of liberation
results. Guilty shame and its cause-effect (the deficient activity) are
elevated to the level of lucid representation. Guilty anxiety ceases to
be a vague feeling and is exposed to the analysis that separates it into
its two factors of imaginative anxiety and real guilt since the anxiety-
laden disorientation is thus overcome by avowal, guilt (purified of ob-

sessive anxiety) objectified and reexposed to the conscious control that is enriched by self-experimentation and by the knowledge of the disastrous consequences of repression. The introspective experience thus restores the superconscious warning—the guilty feeling—in full strength, by elevating the more or less vague feeling to the level of spiritual clairvoyance, spurring the revaluation of meaningless conduct, and the attainment of higher values.

The evolutionary, liberating way of one individual remains valid for all individuals and the species. It determines the guiding values. The mythical consciousness[2] is transformed into psychological science. Based on the cleansing experience, psychology will be capable of piercing the enigmatic facade of extraconscious onirism and of understanding the meaning of the symbolic language of the mythical dream as well as dreams and subconscious pathological oniricism. Self-experience leads to the healing experience. *To heal the sick in spirit*, the producer of psychopathic symptoms, *is to lead him back to the immanent meaning of life*.

The cure, while it replaces the false disharmonizing valuations with harmonizing valuations, reaches, moreover, the deeper subconscious layers from which onirically disguised symptoms emerge, by releasing guilty anxiety. Following repeated repressions, the obsessed conscious is swamped by the subconscious. The call of guilty anxiety is choked by incessant self-justifications. The goal of the cure is to obtain for the patient the ability to hear again and support the call of the superconscious, which stigmatizes the cause of the spirit's illness, the escape into the imaginative exaltation of desires (whether pseudo-spiritual, material, or sexual). The cure, since it opposes repressing justification, successfully penetrates the depth where the repressed desires, anxieties, and their symbolically masked reappearance are generated. Insofar as false justifications cease to feed neurotic symptoms, these gradually disintegrate. The energy of false justification—which fed the formation of symptoms—is drawn forth from its subconscious refuge as the functional significance of the symptom is unveiled: the false promise of satisfaction. By being aware of it, the conscious spreads its domain and its power of control toward the subconscious. The subject liberates himself thanks to the evolutionary impulse that awakens from its dozing—the only essentially valid cure.

The complementary knowledge of the significance of mythical symbolism favors the disappearance of psychopathic symptoms because the symbology in all its forms—including dreams—expresses the essential theme of psychic life, the conflict between the superconscious

warning of guilty anxiety and the subconscious tendency of vain false
self-justification.

*   *   *

It is not superfluous to emphasize that mythical prevision—in what
concerns the modalities of its historical constitution—is the result of a
long adaptive work that proved vital even after the advent of the superconscious (just like animal instinct doesn't all instantly acquire its
precision or its multiform wealth. The sureness of the unconscious,
which is partially disturbed by the evolutionary emergence of the conscious instance and its hesitancy of choice, is reconstituted into superconscious foresight only after long gropings from the premythical
period of *animism*.

Since its origin, the human species can neither satisfactorily survive nor overcome vital restlessness without the elaboration of a directing vision in relation to the meaning of life. As they unify the members
of the individualized species into a common belief, these directing
visions are of a religious order (*religare* = retie, or reharmonize). The
most primitive form of religious life and the product of a psyche in the
process of gestation, the unconscious of which is not differentiated
enough into superconscious and subconscious, *the animist vision*
recalls the psychopathic productions of exalted imagination, with the
difference however, that, far from being a morbid phenomenon of individual regression, animism is a primitive means of collective adaptation.

Only by successive development, superconscious imagination,
which is fully recovering its instinctive sureness, knew how to create
the myths of all peoples that could determine the emergence of great
ancient cultures whose influence extends to the present time. This influence is not only of a collective order; it is also individual in nature.
The animist and mythical layers continue to survive in the extraconscious of the species despite its progressive intellectualization. Thus
mythical images do not cease to animate the subconscious of each individual with their directing force (like animist magic, while degener-
ated into superstitious taboo, has not ceased to exert its influence). The
collective hold of conventional taboos is added and is opposed to intimate determination through guilty anxiety.

From the mythical dream social traditions, morals, and customs
were developed in each nation. Guilt itself has partly deviated from its
essential characteristic of instinctivity. It is attached to social institutions. This deviated form is not even worth the name "guilt." It is only

a specific manifestation of accidental anxiety over the environment, the anxiety over the opinion of fellow creatures, over sanctions or disgrace, inflicted by communities for each breach of tradition. Public opinion is subdivided into ideological traditions (theological, political, and pseudoartisic) that result in the awakening of pseudoguilt on the occasion of each violation of the adopted belief. Insofar as the individual wins intensity, his credulous attachment to conventions diminishes. Also, the more liberated he is from pseudoguilt, the more intense in him is the essential force to admit error in relation to the superconscious instinctivity, which has remained unharmed.

*   *   *

Mythologies or the superconscious productions of ancient times contain an underlying psychological prescience because their common theme is guilty anxiety, which—also of superconscious origin—is the essential, always current, and daily renewed problem of each individual's life. In summary, psychic functioning consists of a constant *deliberation regarding guilty anxiety* that leads either to sublimation or to repression.

Mythically speaking, guilty anxiety is the message of beneficial dieities residing in the higher realms, which are figurative of the superconscious (Olympus, Heaven). The divinities symbolize the various forces (virtues) or the fighting impulses that animate and inspire man (fighting hero) in his battle (psychic conflict) against the subconscious forces (demons and monsters).

The repression of guilty anxiety is the essential defeat.

The punishment symbolically inflicted by deities is a result of essential defeat or the ambivalent demoralization that leads to both forms of illness of the spirit: neurosis (an excess of guilty mortification) and banalization (the devastation of the superconscious sphere and its essential combative impulse). In this sense, morals are not a rigid duty that is contrary to human nature and imposed by divinities. Morals that are a duty, the displeasing moralism, originate in the misunderstanding of the symbolism of myths.

Authentic morals are based upon the dynamism of the evolutionary impulse, the symbols of which are divinities. The immanent ethos is the mysterious vital force that biogenetically became human superconsciousness. The ethos that is an integral part of the deliberating functioning of the psyche is determined by the most characteristic trait of all forms of life, whether preconscious or conscious: the search for satisfactions. As a result of the explosion of elementary drives into a multitude of promises of satisfaction that are vitally valid or nonvalid, superconsciously or subconsciously determined and determining, the deliberating choice acquires its ethical quality as it progressively and successfully discriminates the values from the nonvalues and as it favors pleasures in their natural and sublime forms over the temptations of perverse pleasure.

Pleasure is natural when it is content with the elementary satisfaction of driving appetites which diversify into material and sexual desires. Perverse pleasure seeks an excessive multiplication of desires, the imaginative reveries or banal amusement. The sublime pleasure is joy, the harmony of desires. Sublime pleasure, which is cleansed of perversions, bears satisfaction to its highest degree of intensity.

Only natural desires are harmonizable. Once they are liberated from exaltation, they harmonize on their own, for the demand of harmony is biologically elementary, while the temptation of perverse pleasure or unhealthy distortion, the principle of evil, appears only belatedly at the human level.

The imperative of harmonization is a special case of the evolutionary law of differentiation and integration. To differentiate appetites into multiple desires demands a harmonious reintegration. At the human level, evolutionary finalism becomes *ethical law*.

The biogenesis of the ethical law decides the destiny of humankind, the thinking animal. The individual is free to do and to think what he pleases, but if he wants to be satisfied with himself and his life—each one's essential desire—he ought to submit himself deliberately to the law that demands the harmonious re-integration of multiple desires.

The unique salvation of the individual consists of veraciously thinking his life, which is impossible without the intimate battle against subconscious blinding. Victory is never perfect. To be free from all neurosis and all banalization is impossible; we can only seek harmony, which is unstable by definition and ceaselessly needs to be reestablished.

Because of the immanent failing in human nature, the ethical law assumes the function *of a guiding ideal*. It is the very essence of an ideal to not be perfectly attainable but to inspire the effort of perfecting.

Ethics are the accomplishment of the essential effort. *Authentic ethics are the executive of ethical law*. They are opposed to moralizing convulsion and banal looseness, as well. Ethics are everyday hygiene, as prophylactic and natural as bodily hygiene. In that sense, ethics represent the pleasure of washing oneself. Psychic dirtying is guilty self-dissatisfaction, which is provoked by the impurity of perverse pleasure. Ethics are the cleansing revaluation of promises of satisfaction. Psychic hygiene becomes habit and pleasure, which is derived from the prevision of the unhealthy results of a false pleasure tied to slovenliness. Ethical pleasure needs to be supported and sharpened by a deep knowledge and by a psychic science that can foresee disastrous consequences, such as the insanity of morals-duty and banal cynicism.

Ethics is the economy of pleasure.

Ethical law establishes the unquestionable truth that the ideal of life is the sublimated pleasure called "joy." The terms *joy* and *love of life* are equivalent. One can love life only insofar as one meets the immanent conditions of joy.

Nutrition and sexuality are basic values, for without their satisfaction life cannot continue. Still, material and sexual desires should be sanely valuated, neither overvaluated nor undervaluated, neither exalted nor inhibited. Their sane valuation is the work of the spirit.

But the spirit can overvaluate itself, and this leads to the devaluation of sexuality and materiality. Pseudospirituality destroys the economy of satisfactions and the scale of values by pretending that the search for natural pleasure is a hedonism not worthy of humans. But what is this exalted indignation based on, if not upon the pleasure sought for in the pseudodignity of moralism? Pseudodignity enjoys condemning and blocking *actions* that it considers improper while it gives free rein to imaginative presatisfactions that, because they are shamefully hidden, will not fail to motivate, sooner or later, the collapse of overly good intentions. Instead of mobilizing the autonomous, sanely valuating force of the spirit, the only efficient barrier against the banal and banalizing overvaluation of sexual and material desires, moralism anxiously barricades itself against temptations, in remembrance of all past failures. By perverse pleasure of self-justification (supported by the misunderstanding of mythical symbology) moralism declares that joy is accessible only after death, that life here on earth is a valley of tears and vain repentance, that only supernatural help could protect the innate weaknesses of human nature against the assault of the banal exaltation of "carnal" desires.

Ethics become unauthentic and are lost in ambivalence (moralism-amoralism) as soon as their biogenetic origin is misunderstood. Ethical law and its executive, the ethical code, are products of the evolution of the psyche.

The immoral error consists of introducing a supernatural causation (by taking the mythical image for a logical concept) or a subnatural
causation (which degrades humans into automatons) into the natural
phenomenon that is the splendor of life.

No determining discrimination, no deliberation could be possible
without the premium of an anticipated pleasure. Banalism anticipates
pleasure by the exclusive satisfaction of material and sexual desires.
It seeks justification by asserting that neither good nor evil exists.
Guilty anxiety would be only a pathological error. The lack of scruples
becomes an ideal. The wisdom of language stigmatizes banal amoralism by the terms *platitude, baseness*, and even *ignoble* (absence of
nobility). The term used here, *banalization*, does not include affective
depreciation. It objectively verifies the existence of a banalizing dynamism: The banalized individual falls beneath his innate value, beneath the level of his animating impulse.

Banalization usually escapes diagnosis. Because of its frequency,
it is taken for a norm of social adaptation. The euphoric disinhibition
it proposes is considered a remedy against the excessive inhibition of
moralism. But the banal amoralism, the progressive destruction of the
impulse to transcend, essentially speaking, causes a society's inability
to adapt to the evolutionary meaning of life.

One who is banalized dehumanizes himself by lack of scruples.
He becomes his own enemy. The culture falls apart. Civilization—the
technical organization of the life of communities—can survive for a
long time. But its decline is manifest. It does not protect individuals
who are banally liberated against collective guilt—which extends to all
aspects of social life.

The determinism of guilty anxiety, the message of the superconscious, persists. It affects more than the intrapsychic relation of the instances, it eventually pervades all interhuman relationships and
therefore attests to the entire scope of ethical imperative and its immanent origin. Mythical prescience denounces banalization as a danger greater than neurotic psychopathy, although both are the result of
imaginative exaltation of desires that triggers conflict between the instances and between humans.[3]

In all times, half-conscious thought, impressed by the enigma of
mythical images, strove to elaborate explanatory ideologies. These attempts—already mentioned—were inevitable. Their goal was to safeguard the productions of mythical superconsciousness from oblivion,
in order to impress the crowd of believers and to reunite them with a

common hope that can overcome the vital restlessness and the resulting anxietudes. But it is also inevitable that, ignorant of extraconscious functioning and its symbolic language, these ideologies (philosophical as well as theological)—the traditional determining factors of
the lives of individuals and societies—remained inadequate.

The effort of liberation from the essential error is observable in
all cultures and all epochs. The growing anxiety of disorientation imposes the elucidation of the essential problem, which is the theme of
myths. It can be found only in the clear distinction of the two aspects
of superconscious prevision: the symbolic facade and its underlying
significance, the immanent ethical responsibility.

A. RESPONSIBILITY

The economy of satisfaction first concerns deliberating self-determination, the intrapsychic relation between instances and the relation
of one to oneself. But humans live in society. The most irritating disturbances emanate from the actions of others, especially when wrongly motivated and vainly justified. These relationships cause accidental
anxietude, which is concentrated into guilty anxiety insofar as the subject, who is unable to master the accidents, is psychically traumatized.
In everyone, self-mastery or traumatizing rumination prepares the
sublime or perverse motives of future activity. Each subject becomes a
source of pleasing or displeasing excitations for others.

Mutual displeasing excitations engender hate. Pleasing interreactions are favorable to the deconvulsion of egocentricity at various
degrees of intensity: cordiality, friendship, or love. One can love another insofar as one attains self-mastery, the *sublime dissolution of resentments*. Love, as a feeling, is rejoicing for the individual; as an action, it
becomes rejoicing for social life.

The biologically founded ethical imperative includes the demand
to harmonize interhuman relationships. To overcome hate (the excessive differentiation between the ego and the other) is not sentimental
altruism, but a responsibility based on the economy of pleasure. By as-
suming the essential responsibility, the individual frees himself from
sentimental self-pity, the other ambivalent pole of which is the hateful
indictment of others. Irritating accidents, however, that are brought
about by the environment also give rise to the other aspect of perverse
ambivalence, vain self-justification, and its counterpole of repressed
guilt. Vanity is repressed guilt. It separates, in turn, into the vain, excessive self-condemnation of the neurotic, which is ambivalently con-

trasted by the excessive banal condemnation of others. The ambivalence of "vanity/repressed guilt" rejoins the other perverse pair of "accusation/sentimentality" (excessive hate and hypocritical love). The decomposition of values into ambivalence is lawful, for it is subject to the ethical law that rules disharmonies as well as harmonies.

Ambivalent decomposition gradually extends to all qualities and to all spiritual, material, and sexual desires. It constitutes a *false calculus of satisfaction*. It is false in relation to the value of satisfactions; and it is precise because it is subject to the law of ambivalence. Psychology is responsible for uplifting the subconsciously obsessing calculus to the threshold of the conscious, to make it consciously and knowingly controllable. Vain egocentricity diminishes as the individual—for his own good—assumes his own responsibility.

The tendency, proper to each individual, to withdraw from essential responsibility is the reason society is based on laws that are outwardly imposed and the justice of which is necessarily imperfect. These laws were created to dam up the accidental anxiety coming from the social milieu, but, because of their imperfection, they eventually become the principal cause of the ruling injustice that ranges from mutual accusation and the revolt of the disadvantaged classes to conflicts between nations. For social life, official institutions are less important than the insidiously hidden motivations of individuals.

The belief in individual irresponsibility and the fundamental injustice of life is the cause-effect of the growing injustice that manifests in the form of mutual aggression, on the social level. Viewed from an essential perspective, the debasing consequences are the sanction inflicted by the law of responsibility. As one feels exposed to the unjust assault of others, one ceaselessly complains about it, and one's false justification draws from the common injustice an argument of self-excuse that is apparently valid. Nonetheless, one's value resides in one's adaptation to reality, such as it exists, and in the force of resistance that can oppose perverse influence. Viewed essentially, one—even though exposed to the displeasing excitations of the irritated or anxiety-laden discharge of others—remains responsible for the influence one undergoes and for the weakness that prevents escape from the common, perverse encircling. (It is the significance of the hidden meaning of all nations' mythologies.)

Immanent justice results from the law of responsibility. Each action—but also each feeling, each imagination, and each thought—becomes the determining motive that extraconsciously influences the positive or negative constellation of the psyche. The myth indicates this by the symbol of the "all-seeingness" of the divinity who judges human beings according to their secret intentions. In reality, reward and punishment result from the meaningful or meaningless attitude of the individual toward superconscious guilty anxiety.

Responsibility is an unquestionable law, for, beyond any discussion, it is verified by the balance or unbalance of the individual, by joy (the feeling of one's force in action), or by anxiety (the exact measure of the inadequacy of the vital force and of the lack of intensity of the essential desire and its impulse to surpass).

B. THE INTROSPECTIVE METHOD

Mythical images, the guide of deliberation, are necessarily elaborated from superconsciously instinctive *introspection*, for they contain a psychological prescience. As their secret sense is the truth that presides over life—the immanent justice and individual responsibility—the images that instinctively created and understood by the souls of primitive peoples had the power to fight the tendency of irresponsibility, and thus have a positive effect on each one's deliberation. As progressive intellectualization prevails over the sublime imagination of myths, the guiding images lose their suggestive power. Abandoned by the superconscious and its instinctive prescience, and inadequately guided by the cognition that is preoccupied with adaptation to the environment, the imagination has free rein to be exalted or perverted. Even cognition is affected. Its perspicacity becomes obsessed. Swamped by anxiety that results from imaginative exaltation, the function of understanding that seeks solutions exalts its characteristic trait of being preoccupied with the environment.

The environmental milieu is supposed to be the unique source of satisfaction, or disarray. This supposition will not fail to be promoted to the rank of a supposedly objective theory. In accordance with its primitive function of exploration, cognition exclusively exerts itself to ameliorate environmental conditions. The faculty, positive in itself, to invent utilitarian techniques is pressed into the service of discharging imaginatively exalted desires.

Enslaved by perverse imagination in its form of evasion, cognition creates new temptations and new sources of anxietude. It would be useless to fight the growing anxiety with a half-imaginative, half-cognitive return to the belief in superconscious images. As the capacity to understand and instinctively experience them is irremediably lost, cognition that is adapted to reality can only view the symbolism of

guiding images as plain reality. Literally understood, symbols completely lose their power of superconscious orientation. Belief in the
reality of images engenders its ambivalent counterpole of skepticism.
In this falsely motivated situation, only one remedy exists, to return to
introspection and make it a method of conscious exploration.

The transformational dynamism of anxiety in its evolutionary
form will sooner or later mobilize liberating determination. The law of
responsibility eventually will request cognition *knowingly* to take on
the rectifying control once exerted by mythical superconsciousness.

However long it may take the necessary evolutionary epoch to
break the persistence of traditions, the explaining spirit must successfully understand the enigmatic meaning of its own symbolic productions. If these productions of the superconscious spirit contain an
underlying introspective prescience, then the meaning of life could as
well be put in a psychological formula and could be transformed into
an introspective science capable of deciphering the myths and recovering—condensed into conceptual language—the essential truth that
guided ancient cultures. As the misunderstanding of mythical images
is the cause of the downfall of ancient cultures, the culture of the future, which is knowingly based on the knowledge of the immanent
meaning of life, will necessarily have an increased chance to resist
moralizing and banalizing dangers, the causes of cultural downfall.
What can hope be based upon, if not on the immanent evolutionary
necessity that demands that a physical, systematically established
science be completed by a psychological science based on introspection,
the sole method capable of studying anxiety and its transformational
dynamism. Instead of wasting time only elucidating environmental
randomness or elaborating metaphysical speculation, conscious understanding—in the service of the essential desire—will actively orient toward the meaning of life: Its introspective control will attempt to
achieve the harmony of desires, with the aim of conserving pleasure
and condensing it into joy, instead of wasting it in self-indulgence.

To attempt to foresee the future of evolution is to expose oneself
to the accusation of being utopic, if not downright prophetic. The truth
is that utopia consists of wanting the aim without mobilizing the
means, or of being deluded about the difficulty and scope of the effort.
Foresight in relation to the means and difficulty of realization is the
property of science, and its highest quality. Foresight is valid provided
it is based upon the totality of observed phenomena, which, in the matter of evolution, can be summarized by the progression toward the
lucidity of spirit. No theory of evolution can do without a prevision of

the future. The mechanist transformism leads to a prevision that is a dead end and at best only a wager. It is obliged to pretend that the human species and the current psychophysical organization it has reached is the conclusion of adaptive progression and the final aim of evolution. If evolution is viewed only as a morphological phenomenon—to the exclusion of its psychic aspect—it is obviously impossible to foresee any transformation of the living organism without falling into the unprovable and the absurd. Is not the fact that the absurd appears when the doctrine envisions the future proof that the absurd is already contained in the manner of perceiving the past?

It is only from the past of the psyche that it becomes possible to proceed by extrapolation. The evolutionary curve is determined by its abscissa (the anxiety to overcome) and its ordinate (adaptation by the means of progressive elucidation). At the human level, the necessity of a reflexive orientation appears with the conscious instance. The new "organs" to be created are ideological. The transformation no longer affects the somatic organism as a whole, but solely the nervous system and particularly the brain.

Anxiety has become an intrapsychic danger, and adaptation is accomplished by means of elucidating deliberation. The most destructive danger is to make an error of deliberation—affective blinding—that is likely to falsify the elements of the deliberating calculus—the motives—by way of repression. In relation to this intrapsychic complication and its destructive threat, adaptive orientation has remained at the groping level and proceeds by the primitive method of trial and error. Even ideologies are a result of this groping. It is perfectly foreseeable, by extrapolation of evolutionary direction, that what conscious life has acquired—the lucid orientation toward the outer world—will be completed, in order to ward off intrapsychic danger, with a new "organ" capable of ideological rather than perceptive elucidation: the *inner sight*, the aptitude for self-observation and self-control.

One should view this foresight as a hypothesis. It is founded on the laws that rule the insanity and the sanity of psychic functioning.

* * *

The necessity of a cleansing introspection has been recognized from the beginning of extraconscious psychology. About this subject, Freud (1950) mentions, "When you have acquired a certain self-discipline and you possess the appropriate knowledge, your interpretations will remain independent of your personal particularities and will hit the mark. I do not say that for this part of the task the personality of the

analyst is indifferent. A certain finesse of ear, so to speak, is required
to hear the language of the repressed unconscious, and everyone does
not possess it to the same degree" (p. 143).

This is the entire problem. The "finesse of ear" is an allusion to
introspection as a psychological talent and not as an explicit method.
Indeed, Freudian theory contains right elements precisely because
Freud possessed the "finesse of ear" to a very high degree. His theory
is correct insofar as he based it on a secret introspection, but it remains
mixed with errors because instead of using introspection systematically, he had to be content with tying authentic finds together by a sys-
tematizing speculation. Freud himself foresees the danger: "More than
one psychologist finds the situation hopeless and thinks that any
dummy is entitled to take his own (interpretative) dumbness for wisdom. I admit that I am more optimistic" (p. 184).

The optimism is justified by the understanding of the radical difference between "finesse of ear" and "inner sight." The ear listens to
the justifications of others; finesse more or less perspicaciously discerns true from false. The inner sight sees. But in order to see objectively, it needs the proper lucidity to orient itself in the subconscious
darkness. Conversely, it is impossible to look into another's psyche and
to pierce the obscuration. Objective lucidity toward others is impossible without a preliminary objectification toward oneself; only inner
sight—methodical introspection—is suitable to acquisition of a veracious knowledge of psychic intimacy. This knowledge can be used—by
projection—for the objective explanation of the psychic constellation of
another. Falsely justifying introspection of our own motives is the
cause of the morbid interpretation of motives and actions of others.

*Any interpretation, whether right or false, of the motives of others
is based on projective introspection.* It is not the finesse of ear but the
degree of lucidity of the inner sight concerning one's own motives that
makes one fit to understand the secret motives of others and to help
them cleanse their own introspection.

In this respect, it cannot be superfluous to recall the inscription
on the front of the Temple of Apollo, the god of health and harmony:
"Know thyself." The condition of harmony, that is to say, psychic
health, is *self-knowledge*.

*   *   *

Elucidating introspection becomes impossible only at an overly advanced degree of banalization when the fault that is indicated by guilty anxiety is once and for all transformed into euphoric vanity.

Banalization and neurosis are pathological attempts to establish harmony or agreement with oneself by repressing the intimate discord of guilty anxiety. They attain only a dissatisfying pseudoharmony.

The banalized individual's introspection is reduced to a work of deliberation that entirely lacks fullness and essential impulse and only more or less envisions cunning and down-to-earth intentions of discharge. His intellectual lucidity is often great, but it is deprived of spirituality (the orientation toward the meaning of life). The introspection of the neurotic is constant but morbid, and it rarely finds the way to elucidation; the neurotic attempts to reestablish agreement with himself by muffling the displeasure of guilt through fallacious pleasures that are drawn from his exaltation toward the spirit. The intellect of the neurotic is easily obsessed by imaginative escapes, while his spirituality, often intense, exhausts itself in the pursuit of pseudoidealist rambles that are condensed into an exalted task. That's why the neurotic type frequently excels in pseudospiritual productivity (ideological, artistic, and so on). He seeks a substitute for the essential production, which he neglects and which is the formation of the character, specifically the intrapsychic arrangement that is the condition of all authentic spiritual activity.

Everyone is more or less affected by the banal and neurotic forms of deformation; because humans belong to a half-conscious species that, in its present state of development, is inadequately provided with "inner sight" and, therefore, the ever increasing intrapsychic danger will eventually demand the adaptive effort of intimate exploration. Biologically speaking, resistance to the evolutionary progression is a natural phenomenon because the effort to surpass is triggered only after the exhaustion of other adaptative means, also in animals. *Life is characterized by the tendency to preserve acquired forms as well as by evolutionary growth.* It is as if nature—to open up in all multiformity—"wanted" to experiment with all the manifestations of life, anxiety with its suffering as well as the surpassing and satisfaction. The surpassing occurs only if the anxiety is paramount. In this respect, neurosis and banalization can be viewed as a means of adaptation in its conservative form. Their resistance to the awareness of intrapsychic danger could be an attempt to protect against the evolutionary demand and its difficult accomplishment. Vain satisfaction—which is banally euphoric or neurotically exalted—manages to hold guilty dissatisfaction in check, somehow, and renders the half-conscious state that is actually realized by the species bearable. But on the other hand, its destructive misdeeds are prepared in the subconscious. Thus, the subconscious itself would serve the vital impulse that demands surpassing because the destructive power of the subconscious—the ambivalent decomposition of values—will eventually force the conscious to accept the salutary message of the evolutionary instance of the superconscious.

However, this understanding will be capable of creating the "new organ"—the inner sight or introspective lucidity—with the sole condition that the accidental discovery and acknowledgment of guilt be supported by the comprehension of the lawfulness of psychic functioning, *by the knowledge of the roots and effects of perverse and sublime pleasure*, of repression and sublimation-spiritualization. The comprehension of satisfying or dissatisfying consequences is alone capable of unbalancing the half-conscious deliberation definitely to the side of acknowledgment of guilt, which seems distressing but is, in truth, liberating.

Psychological science, anxious to establish an introspective method, is therefore a beginning step in the dawning evolutionary course. At best, its effort possesses only the scope of a first, isolated variation. At the animal level, there is an entire evolutionary epoch between the manifestation of this first indication and the adaptive transformation of the species. Therefore, the resistance to this form of "variation" that is represented by the method of scientific introspection is natural. This resistance itself is a phenomenon of anxiety. It comes from the fear that objectivity, which is the sovereign value of science, could be questioned by the adoption of a method that is appropriate to the observation of the subject. The truth is the psychic state plays an important role even in physics, where the most appropriate method consists of outer observation. The interpretation of observed phenomena is here also essential; banalizing conformism and vain resistance against innovation are the most frequent obstacles of progress. The ultimate criterion of objectivity remains an orderly affectivity. *All arguments that pretext an impossible introspective method are, in the end, attributable to the fact that the anxiety to be confronted is an anxiety-laden problem*. To take seriously the problem of anxiety, to pursue it to its real lair, asks us suddenly to confront our own anxiety and essential danger.

Intrapsychic anxiety exists, and it is contrary to the spirit of sciences to renounce its elucidation. How could science be disinterested by a human being assaulted by anxiety? How could science admit it is disarmed and take the side of repressing anxiety against elucidating spirit?

This forsaking would eventually concern science and its theory and practical life as well, in its most essential aspect, the intrapsychic battle between the subjective blinding of anxiety and objective clairvoyance of spirit. The intrapsyche is not a static object, but the very center of the dynamism of life. The most frequent objection to the possibility of lucid introspection refers to this dynamic fluctuation of the intrapsyche. But the ceaseless liability of psychic content and its fluctuation between meaningful and meaningless truly are the highest justification of intimate observation and the statement of its necessity. Without the fluctuating dynamism of the psyche, introspection would be exerted at a loss; it would not produce an observable effect, morbid or healing. Because it is the nature of motives to be transformed from sublime into perverse and from perverse into sublime, introspection, by becoming objective, acquires a practical scope; it transforms sickness of the spirit into psychic health. It is the evolutionary principle that has been elevated to a method. As it produces observable effects, intimate observation is also an experimentation. Introspection, insofar as it is methodically liberated from anxiety-laden affectivity, assumes all demands of "scientificness"; it is experimental and teachable.

Even though deprived of a method, this experimental observation has been used intuitively in all ages. Because of it, men, who are endowed with an intense impulse to surpass have successfully transformed pathos into ethos and passive passion into meaningful action. However, the certainty of its validity is difficult to establish, because the individual forces of sublimation, which are too easily swamped by the obsessive forces of perverse anxiety, are inadequately supported by the spiritualizing effort of science.

*   *   *

Psychology will live up to its name and become a genuine science of the psyche and its functions, only on the condition that it confronts the problem of intrapsychic anxiety. It is not exempted from elevating the fundamental phenomenon of human life, guilty anxiety and its determining power, to the station of a problem. The determinism of anxiety extends its domination over the realm of science. It is composed of repressive and elucidative forms. The repressive form causes science to retreat from the study of the intrapsyche; as an elucidative form, it causes the spirit of science to prevail over the anxiety of retreat and psychology eventually to overcome the phobia of this object of study called the subject, by making individual attempts of intimate observation into a real method.

In earlier work, I expounded on the details of the introspective method (see Diel, 1989a). This method, which resulted from an intimate experience, can, without doubt, be perfected. It should not be judged according to any given current ideology, but only after an experimental verification.

As methodical self-observation is an objectifying and teachable experimentation, a therapeutic technique necessarily follows (see Diel, 1989a, chap. 2). In the realm of therapy more than anywhere else, the problem of the method in psychology is acutely posed; each individual is entitled to refuse self-observation, except for the therapist. The observation of others, to be objective, demands that the observer-therapist be gradually freed from blinding affectivity.

If methodical self-observation—or *self-analysis*—were impossible, the analysis of others would also be impossible; any analysis, whether we want it or not, is an inducement addressed to the patient to introspect, to be aware of his faults. An analyst only guides the analysis and self-observation. *What right has the therapist to expect the patient to introspect, if he, the guide, refuses to do it under the pretext that autocontrol is impossible?* To direct retrospective attention toward infantile complexes and past traumas is only a means to camouflage the essential and always current cause of wrong motivation.

However, how could the analyst objectively guide the vital introspective autocontrol of the analysis and, without having first elucidated, in himself, the causes of subjective blindness, the guilty vanity and indicting sentimentality—everyone's secret temptations—because they are the categorical foundation of the calculus of false satisfactions.

In order to acquire a sufficient degree of objectivity, didactic analysis is desirable; but in order to be efficient, should it not be based upon a genuine knowledge of the subconscious calculus of false satisfaction that determines the perversion of psychic functioning? What does the proof of this acquired knowledge consist of, if not of the fact that it confers to the analyzed analyst the aptitude to pursue his own analysis? Nothing is more vain than to believe didactic analysis to be in a position to confer objectivity forever. No one can become perfectly objective, that is to say, totally liberated from the false intrapsychic calculus that seeks satisfaction in repressive anxiety. But it is possible to be gradually free from anxiety, by unrepressing falsely justifying motives, which elevates the subconscious calculus to the position of a knowingly understood psychological calculus that can be used for a gradually more lucid liberation. Unrepression, if it is systematically done according to rule, far from bringing about a loss of time and energy, reduces the squandering of affective disorder (see "Psychological Calculus," in Diel, 1989a). (This squandering is attributable to the transformation of deliberation into imaginative rumination. Deliberation revolves and turns into rumination insofar as it is unable to control determination through subconscious motives.)

However, aside from the technique of analytical observation, the problem of method in psychology concerns the result to be obtained and the experience of synthesis. The patient suffers from a contradictory valuation, half-subconscious and half-superconscious, the obsessive opposition of which prevents him from reaching a harmonizing synthesis on the conscious plane. Since psychic health exists as a function of right valuations, therapy can be efficient only insofar as it successfully eliminate the erroneous valuation, the false justification (which grafts pseudosublime motives onto subconscious and perverse motives). As morbid anxiety results from the contradictory valuation that leads to the ambivalence of feelings, the healing experience—the synthesis to be obtained—is inseparably bound to the ethical problem that concerns the scale of values.

C. THE IMMANENCE OF VALUES

The preceding developments were intended to demonstrate that human life, which is determined by the evolutionary law of differentiation-reunification, is valid insofar as people can authentically liberate themselves from anxiety-laden dissatisfaction and especially from its essential form of guilty anxiety. *The effort of liberation is not imposed by any principle that is foreign to human nature.* Its value, of immanent origin, comes from the fact that it is impossible to live adequately in the state of guilty disunion and that the progressive disunion of the disassociation of the psyche is an effect of an unauthentic liberation—a denying of guilt. *The analysis of anxiety is therefore summarized and culminates in the problem of the immanent value of satisfying liberation.* This is why it was necessary to develop—even though in a fragmented manner—the problem of values throughout this exposition, the goal of which consists of establishing the distinction between the two forms of anxiety (evolutionary and involutionary). Once at the culminating point, it is important to reassemble the dispersed elements in order to sketch a comprehensive view of the problem of values. The most economical way to accomplish this is to sum up the stages of analysis that are necessary for the synthesis, even at the cost of certain repetition.

The need to seek satisfaction is the common link among all living species, whether higher or lower. This common vital demand originally concerns the preservation (nutrition and reproduction) of the somatic organism; already in its most elementary aspect, the immanent imperative is primarily *psychic in nature*, since the dissatisfaction to overcome is immediately felt in the form of an emotional tension. Therefore, the need for satisfaction determines the indivisible totality of the psychosomatic organism.

This elementary need also determines the organo-psychic evolution, the means to guarantee life preservation in the event of persistent dissatisfaction. Evolution is a special case of the basic need for self-preservation. It attempts to preserve life even if the species in its current form is exposed to mortal danger because of environmental disfavor. The anxiety-laden dissatisfaction transforms the elementary, in itself, static need for preservation into dynamic surpassing. The surpassing is evolutionary, because it imperturbably follows the ascent to ever more lucid functions of orientation. Immanent finalism manifests in animals as an unconscious thrust that can create always more efficient means of satisfaction that are, on the psychic plane, the various functions of instinctive preorientation somatically provided with executive organs capable of perceptive elucidation. Already at this still preconscious level, the evolutionary growth contains an element of prospection (the spirit), which deserves to be accredited with higher value than the conservative nutritional and sexual satisfactions. This first indication of a higher value of the functions of orientation (instinctivity and perceptivity) in relation to elementary and conservative drives (nutrition and sexuality) is at this preconscious level still very clearly limited to a phenomenon of pure immanence: to the fact that the *elucidating prospection assures its most efficiently satisfying means to evolutionary adaptation.* At the human level, higher satisfaction, because it is evolutionary in nature, no longer exclusively depends on either instinctive prevision or perceptive orientation. The evolutionary growth, by unfolding all its demands of ascent toward lucidity, is metamorphosed into spiritual drive. From instinctive and perceptive, prevision becomes selective and valuating.

Yet, valuation does not create values. They preexist because of their preconscious immanence and their genetic unfolding.

The conflict-filled situation of humans is characterized by the fact that they are the sole living beings having the leisure to follow the slant of involution that leads to the exaltation of desires to the extent that any true satisfaction becomes impossible. Because of the conflict that opens thus within this vital center—the need for satisfaction—the biological value acquires the range of a directive ideal.

The ideal is ethical in nature, it implies a duty and it is objectively valid because of the immanent factor of satisfaction, which is difficult for the individual to attain. This duty imposes nothing but what every individual essentially desires at the very depth of his nature and with his extraconscious root in the biological foundation of life. The duty consists of liking one's essential self sufficiently to be capable of attaining one's own higher interest, the harmonious satisfaction of all meaningful desires that is the condition of joy (sublimating egoism). Evil—the imaginative blinding of valuating lucidity—is opposed to this essential good.

Good and evil, far from being ethical entities that exist independent of human nature, are reduced—in a biological sense—to the good and evil that humans do to themselves (which is only another expression of the law of economy that implies responsibility and immanent justice).

Ethical law has more than a subjective reach. It is impossible to love one's essential self without being detached from the egotist form of self-love. Authentic self-satisfaction is incompatible with vain oversatisfaction and its counterpole of guilty dissatisfaction. Objectivity toward oneself, which ethical law imposes, renders one objective toward others.

As the evolving subject becomes objective and realizes the value of life, so others cease to be objects of his need for triumph and revenge. Self-love, taken to a sufficient degree of concentration and efficiency, surpasses the ego and becomes, as a result of its objectivation, a kind of energetic radiation that is at the opposite of restrictive hatred and sentimental effusion as well. This stems from the biological origin of vital energy—the product of retention—for energy is, from the beginning, magnetized toward the world. At the human level, the evolved retention manifests as intimate deliberation, the intrapsychic work exerted on motives in which retentional energy is differentiated.

*   *   *

There isn't and there cannot exist any other means to liberate retained energy and to carry it to the degree of intensity where it becomes heat and radiation other than to love oneself deeply enough to aspire actively to the essential satisfaction that leads back to the biologically primary demand of a harmonious relation with the environment, by a harmonious accord with the ego.

But where is the individual who can, without fail, prefer inner success to material success and the satisfaction of ambitions that make him dependent upon the social world, its promises and its disappointments—the external goals of the disagreement between individuals? *The scale of values* is established insofar as individual valuation remains oriented toward authentic inner success. The values are graded from primitive material need to degrees of attraction that are higher in intensity of satisfaction, and culminate in an ideal that exerts an attractive force but is not attainable in itself: the lovingness that is purified of all subjective and exclusive attachment.

The scale of values defines the positive qualities of psychic intimacy (the harmony of motives) and the positive qualities of active behavior as well (a meaningful relationship with others). *The immanence of the values creates psychology and sociology.* The qualities are felt and viewed as positive by the subject who emits them as well as by the other who is the receptor-object. The subject feels the value of his own existence insofar as he feels in harmonious agreement with himself; others judge the harmonized subject satisfying because his activity is free from vexatious intentions. (The value of others, though, should not be felt as a vexation, as this is an error of judgment that can only be due to one's own nonvalue.) Values, by the rejoicing pleasure they procure for the individual and at a social level, are, by definition, opposed to vital displeasure or anxietude, which, in the scale of values, constitutes the negative degrees that dissatisfy the subject and displease others.

The judgments of values, the motives of actions, are completed with an intimately felt self-judgment. The objective valuation assumes a subjective character of self-estimation. Self-esteem, or justified pride (the opposite of a vain overesteem), is the highest satisfaction par excellence.

In a sanely valuating intrapsyche all the objectifying conditions of the judgment in relation to oneself and others are reunited. They are in the revision of the overvaluation of oneself (vanity) and others (sentimentality) or the devaluation of oneself (guilt) and others (accusation). *The false justification that is composed of overesteem and underesteem of oneself and others, draws all its obsessive determination from the imperative need to reconstitute the immanent value, even if fallaciously, in order not to lose the essential satisfaction of esteem.*

*   *   *

The human being is, among all living beings, the only one who cannot live without self-esteem. However, this self-valuation or self-esteem can be deceptive. In overestimating oneself, one truly loses value. The origin of values and nonvalues is intrapsychic; the cause of nonvalues is not only somatic activity, but also, and especially, mental activity, the wrong motivation. It leads to a false self-valuation of the individual. Its most serious consequence is the false traditional and collective estimation of the problems that impose themselves upon individuals, the most important of which is the problem of values.

All preceding analyses relating to the anxiety of disorientation due to ambivalent (spiritualist and materialist) solutions of the problem of values can be concentrated and summed up into one statement: *the traditional error is based on the ignorance of the extraconscious progression of motivating self-determination.* Whether right or wrong, it decides the value of humankind and the value of theories.

Let traditional mentality introduce the idea of free will or the idea of an automatism deprived of valuating freedom in the place of extraconscious self-determination; the common error is in the devaluation of human nature that is viewed as fundamentally immoral or amoral. Evil, thus conceived, does not occur as an illness of the spirit that is liable to be cured (at least in principle) by objectifying self-revaluation. Evil would be an ineluctably innate weakness, opposed to a principle of good that is represented by supernatural help or social authority. In this wrong point of view, the motive of the good is not the impulse of surpassing, the love of the evolutionary ego. It is not a natural attraction that is sharpened by guilty anxiety, the intrapsychic sanction, but the fear of social or extratemporal sanctions.

The immanent meaning, on the contrary, is evolutionary finalism. It prescribes to life its meaningful direction, its immanent value. The meaning of evolution is to overcome the initial discord between matter and spirit.

The value of human life resides in the effort to surpass the conflicts between material and spiritual desires. Nothing could be more contrary to the immanent meaning and more meaningless than to make this conflict an irreconcilable matter by according an absolute value to either matter or spirit. The idea of a double-edged absolute shapes the immanent value into an ambivalence. It exalts the initial discord rather than conciliating it and introduces it into human thought as a seemingly solutionless dispute.

All of human history is essentially determined by the dispute of ideologies, which could be unimportant if ideas were not essential motives of activities and interactions. The only solution is to revise the guiding motives, the contradiction of which causes anxiety-laden disorientation.

The analysis, to bring out the extent of ambivalences, finds itself in the obligation to portray their excessive manifestations. It is necessary to add that, in reality, valid and nonvalid attitudes interpenetrate and form combinations of an unlimited variability. Every individual is codetermined by one or the other of the ideologies proposed by society, but he remains essentially determined by the force or weakness of the impulse that animates him. Ideological traditions are themselves the product of the impulse of generations seeking support. Each one will opt for a given idealizing doctrine partly due to the randomness of encountered influences, which are, moreover, mostly determined by impositions undergone as early as childhood. Faithfulness to doctrines, however, is not necessarily an indication of conformist weakness. Sometimes, it indicates the intensity of the impulse that seeks the solutions to contradictions while accepting the dogmatic or doctrinal coating.

In all camps there are individuals of generous temperament. The dispersal of combative impulse into more or less conventionalized camps depends upon the historical unfolding, the balance of fanatic idealism and banal intrigue. Still, the history of humanity is essentially determined by the impulse of surpassing, ceaselessly in revolt against indoctrination. Doubtless it has always been understood that unleashed avidity is the result of a disorientation relating to values. Doubtless also, defining the immanent origin of values has been attempted. The research remains arbitrary so long as the nature of the immanence is not established: the intrapsychic conflict of the various ambivalences from which every person suffers, where the harmonious appeasement of the anxiety-laden conflict becomes for everyone— whether he wants it or not—the immanent meaning of his life, and for all humans the guiding value, the ethical law. Because it is so, superconscious instinctivity has always known how to formulate the intrapsychic conflict between values and nonvalues symbolically.

What is likely to change is not the scope of the values, but only the lucidity of formulation that, from implicit and figurative, attempts to become explicit and conceptual. The explanation is necessarily complicated. It should unveil the biogenesis of values (the products of retentional energy) to demonstrate that no one can escape the imperative of values without undergoing the deviation and the lessening of his impulse, which would not be serious if the intensity of individual and collective satisfactions did not depend on the validity of impulses.

The problems of values not only concern life and its value. They imply the mystery of death. The values, their biogenetic demands and their social dogmatizations, cannot be entirely understood if it is not considered that, beyond their ethical reach, they are conceived as a means to overcome *anxiety of death and its mystery*. It is thus not astounding that, outside the mythical symbology relating to this problem, there are attempts of consolation: rites and ceremonies that possess a magically suggestive power. Let us complete the analysis of anxiety (a truly inexhaustible theme) by outlining the collective and social effort to contain anxiety in its most ineluctable form.

NOTES

1. Because of this antithetical relation, mythical symbolism can foresee the danger of subconscious onirism. It is illustrated by the image of the "devouring monster." This image perfectly expresses the psychic phenomenon; the subconscious "devours" vital energy by capturing it and accumulating it in a perverted form. The organism is vitally threatened by this "monstrous" danger, which reaches even its somatic functions. The psychopathic subconscious is the "lair" where lodges the destructive monster (the repressed anxiety). A distortion of the primitive unconscious, the subconscious retains and exaggerates even the tendency to express emotional agitation (now repressed anxiety) by organic disorders.

2. Translator's note: in French, *conscience*.

3. Psychological language, like the mythical dream, uses—to express the conflicting situation of the psyche—the inevitable spatial image. The "more-than-conscious" and the "less-than-conscious" are illustrated by means of a spatial superposition that signifies the superiority or inferiority of the values of satisfaction. The universality of laws that rule the relation of psychic instances is, moreover, emphasized by the comparison with spatial motion of the cosmic universe.

   The sky, where the stars move harmoniously, illustrates the superconscious sphere and its demand for psychic harmony (the illuminating sun becomes symbol of the spirit). The subconscious is represented as the underground domain. (Because of the "night-day," "sun-moon" opposition, a relation is established between the underground and the lunar and the result is that both represent the malefic principle of obsession.) The median sphere of the earth and the habitat of humans and their battle-field symbolize the conscious instance and the conflicts of deliberation.

   The intrapsychic constellation as a whole is thus illustrated by a mythical image. This image becomes metaphysical because, by its analogical development, the symbolization opposes the underground domain (Hell: habitat of maleficent deities) with the superterrestrial domain of the Beyond, where beneficent deities reside (Heaven). According to the mythical image, beneficent deities lend their help (the forces of sublimation-spiritualization) to the individual who is animated with an essential fighting impulse.

As burial is the most frequent funeral custom, the dead, according to mythical imagination, meet the underground and infernal deities who judge their past lives and sanction their failings in the essential battle. Often, also, in opposition to this image, the valiant souls receive their reward in the Beyond and are authorized to sit in Heaven. These eschatological images denote the inexplicable aspect of existence; the impossibility of admitting that life came out of an absolute nothing, leads one to imagine that death is not a simple annihilation. The inexplicable principle of animation is represented by the "soul." The modalities of the survival image are necessarily borrowed from the modalities of psychic life, which vacillates between joy and anxiety.

To the image of the life of the soul after death corresponds the mythical image of a "death of the soul" during life (banalization). Psychologically speaking, the sanction is guilty anxiety and the consequences of its repression, desolation in all its forms, whether nervous or banal. Likewise, the reward that is distributed by the deities is a symbolization of joy that results from harmonization. Mythical superconscious expresses the determining dynamism of instances by symbolically personified images common to all peoples.

8

The Anxiety of Death

At the preconscious level, the fear-terror and the reaction of surrender are triggered by the sudden emergence of a life-threatening danger. The human being, who is capable of scanning the future, becomes aware of his end, which is, inevitably, death. Therefore, anxiety of life-threatening danger is introduced in the very core of life, insofar as it adaptively attempts to become spiritualized. If the imagination of a sure termination does not entirely pervade life with mortal anxiety and does not trigger the reactions of fright and surrender, it is because vital dynamism, while becoming spiritualized, creates the means to spiritualize anxiety of death, to convert it into a metaphysical and sacred feeling. The dreaded threat is not immediately and suddenly presented, and so imagination, instead of taking fright, has the time to realize that death is not only a phenomenon of annihilation, but its inexplicable aspect concerns the beyond of the phenomenon (life and death). Life itself could not exist if the "beyond" of its beginning and end were a void. Death is an existing phenomenon and a mystery as well; it is the event through which, ineluctably, existence is engulfed by the mystery.

Superconscious imagination takes into account the inexplicable aspect of death. In the mythical dream, life is prolonged beyond death. This prolongation, however, is an onirical image that uses temporal duration to express that annihilation of existence cannot be conceived as absolute. The mythical symbol for voidness, which is relative to the temporal, for the extratemporal, inexplicable in itself, is "Eternity."

Immanent values are symbolically transcended by the mythical image of Eternity. In order to understand this figurative transposition, nothing is more important than to perceive the obvious truth that anxiety of death is a manifestation of life. Life and its short duration be-

come anxious in the face of endless death. It is the living being's anxiety that conceives death as an experienced time span and that popu-
lates this endless time span—pure imagination—with idealized beings
fancied as living eternally.

Imagination, a primitive form of elucidating thought, prolongs
life into death and thereby creates the image of a beyond populated by
superhuman beings who are conceived from humankind's meaningful
activity and thus are pictured as judges of the meaningful or meaningless activity of mortal humans. It is conceived that the human rejoins,
after real life, the superhuman beings who live in the *beyond of anxiety*, in the symbolic location of imperishable joy (Heaven); or, the imagination leads to the eternalization of anxiety and creates the symbolic
image of a place where the punishment of meaningless activity is
forever accomplished (Hell). Thus, meaningful activity finds stimulation, and anxiety of death, its appeasement.

*These images are based on elements belonging to apparent reality,
the death phenomenon and superconscious onirism.* Superconscious
symbolism could not be veracious if it weren't the expression of an
analogical relation between these two ends of life: death of individuals
(that leads to the mystery) and species evolution (that leads to the manifestation of values). The symbol allows myths to formulate the understanding that the values upon which the meaning of life evolutionally unfolds also stand for the meaning of the mystery of death.
(As the inexplicable is pictured as the creator principle, its meaning
manifests through the meaningful activity of creation.) The evolutionary manifestation of values (pictured as eternally preexisting)
doesn't exhaust the depth of the unfathomable, but values are viewed
as the apparent clue, the only clue that can be grasped.

The psychological truth of these images, which eternalize life and
its value beyond death, resides not only in the mystery of death, but
also in the fact that the idea of death, already during life, stimulates
the essentially valid effort of harmonization by opposing the exaltation
of desires. *The anxiety of death disappears insofar as humans fulfill life
by their meaningful activity. To fulfill life by realizing its immanent
value of joy is to love life, and this sublimed love of life alone possesses
the power truly to dissolve the anxiety of death. The latter is transformed into sacred anxiety, which no longer fears death of the body but
death of the soul (the destruction of harmony).*

The supreme force of the unified soul—because it is in agreement
with itself—resides in the fact that it is no longer provoked into anxiety by the accidents of life or the seductions and threats coming from

the world, even if mortal. This complete liberation, this serene independence, this supreme pride (entirely based upon active merit and, therefore, exempt of all vain imagination) is, in the psychological sense, the ultimate wisdom of the calculus of satisfaction that leads to the everlasting rest in joy (symbolically called Heaven). *Biologically speaking, the basic need for satisfaction finds its perfect accomplishment by means of the final reversal. The demand for preservation no longer concerns the body but the spirit that animates it. Because of this shift of the significance to the impulse of animation (the most authentic manifestation of the mystery of life and death), the reversal of the principle of satisfaction confers a religious meaning to the ethical ideal.*

The characteristic trait of the religious feeling (as distinct from religion) is—much more than the belief attached to stimulating images—the strength of soul that is capable of operating the essential reversal or, at least, of actively aspiring to it to the extent of its limited strength. Only fortitude of an exceptional potential can perfectly achieve liberation from any anxiety about life and about death, as well. In most cultures, the liberating hero is only a mythical image, a pure symbol. The only ones who actually achieve liberation—Buddha the saved, Christ the savior—remain exemplary and become therefore the crystallizing center of great cultural epochs. Imagination, which is superconscious of the unique value of their accomplishment, symbolically deifies them, thereby reinforcing and eternalizing the suggestive extent of the example, which, from then on, becomes able to create a potentially motivating superconscious focus in fervent souls throughout centuries. The figurative deification is only a means of stimulating the suggestive extent of the exemplary accomplishment (the real meaning of which is victory over banalization during life, "the resurrection of the death of the soul; see Diel, 1986).

Faith is mythically profound only if the belief attached to the metaphysical image remains secondary to the vivifying faith and its activating determination. The evolutionary ideal, the true guide of the species, no longer consists of obtaining the meaningful determination through figurative suggestion, but thanks to this correct valuation of life and death, which, roused by an impulse of exceptional intensity, permits perfect realization of the essential desire. This desire animates each individual in various degrees and attempts to overcome anxiety until death, and attain the ultimate and immanent value of life, joy (a state the perfect degree of which is symbolized by the images of Heaven and Nirvana). The exemplary value of the accomplishment is that it proves that triumph over anxiety is, in principle, not beyond our strength, but included in the possibilities of human nature. This comprehension excludes the risk of taking images for realities, while they can retain their true, meaningful significance. The guide of activity, rather than the onirical superconscious and the historical example (the value of which remains intact), becomes the science of the lawfulness of psychic functioning—of which the superconscious images are the symbol and the most exemplary individual realization of which is only an illustration. To understand lawfulness liberates because it prevents any imitative exaltation, while it mobilizes the impulse to surpass according to its authentic intensity.

Far more frequent than meaningful and conscious liberation from superconscious images is detachment in its meaningless form and subconscious origin: repression of sacred anxiety. *Through this repression, anxiety of death becomes an obsession.* But because of repressive forgetfulness, obsessive anxiety loses its sacred nuance. Anxiety of death is converted into exalted love of life, into a banal activity that clings to life through exaltation of desires. The numerous resulting projects come up against the exalted desires of the many others and their own projects of attainment; therefore, each one's desires are turned into accidental anxiety in the form of hatred, resentment, and worries. Embittered, human becomes the enemy of human. *Collective anxiety, as it loses its sacred nuance, becomes the anxiety of collectivities,* such as it can usually be observed, and no longer concerns the meaning of life, which becomes ineffective in relation to the ever-present insufficiency of institutions that are incapable of staunching the egotist overflow. (Generalized anxiety gives rise to false justifications-accusations of erroneous motivations, the most profound cause of which is intrapsychic anxietude, the repression of the sacred anxiety of death.)

*   *   *

It is not difficult to understand how material miseries are generated from the misery of souls that arises from the stifling of collective anxiety in its sacred form; luxury and lust are the seductive aspects of these miseries. The complication of accidental and essential causes and effects results in the fact that accidental effects, by acting on the psyche, are retransformed into an essential cause, into motives. This is why no accidental and external remedy can be essentially efficient, unless its intention finds support in the conscience of individuals where it arouses the essential remedy: the revision of motives. As long as this retransformation has not occurred, life is not viewed in the intimate feeling as the only opportunity to gain authentic satisfaction, but rather as an oppressive habit. Accidental anxiety obsessively seeks its accidental remedies, and sacred anxiety is awakened only on a few rare occasions, known to all, where, in the face of the threat of a decisive failure, the veil of conventional habit is torn and the vanity of the effort becomes suddenly obvious. The idea of death dawns and, insofar as the essential weakness was great (and provided the essential desire subsists), the exalted love of conventionalized life risks being converted into a suicidal idea, an idea that is the emergence of the fright and surrender reaction. The whole of life becomes problematic; the problem of the value or nonvalue of life in general and the individual's life becomes heavy.

* * *

The subconscious conversion of sacred anxiety into accidental anxietude, the attempt to forget through conventional agitation and the resulting fight of everyone against everyone are the principal causes of the progressive decomposition of cultural communities. It is why, to control danger and to conjure away anxietude, all communities, since the most remote times, first sought the remedy in *the dogmatic reinforcement of their mythical foundation.*

In all mythically founded communities, metaphysical and moral theories are thus generated from superconscious guiding images. Before they became philosophical and abstract, the attempts at explanation possessed a theological character, remaining gathered around symbols that personified immortal deities.[1]

The idea that these deities really exist and really intervene in the lives of humans, exerts a profound influence on the life of collectivities. *It changes all the data of the problem of collective anxiety.* The link uniting members of the community, which was originally constituted by the authentic superconscious vision and its instinctive determination, is gradually more externalized and socialized. The religious institution becomes the support of the belief and is in charge of the task of conjuring away anxiety by means of the cult. The significance is little by little transposed from meaningful activity to ritual actions and ceremonies of the cult, and it is eventually first and foremost the participation in the cult that assures the favor of the real deities during life and after death. The belief in the real existence of the "Immortals" implies the belief in a real immortality. The myth—the basis of religious institutions—symbolized the values of life and the mystery of death, as well. It had no other way to speak of the indefinable extratemporal than to represent "Eternity," symbolic image, as an infinite duration. Theological ideologies of all peoples—taking the symbol literally—create thus the consoling belief that humans will participate in immortality after death, immortality taken as a reality. Social anxiety (the intrapsychic anxiety heightened by social injustice) seeks appeasement in the belief of a compensating justice in the beyond. Consolation, however, makes one lose sight of the essential psychic truth, superconsiously proposed by mythical images, which is the immanence of values and the inherence of justice, the only genuine palliative of anxiety in all its forms: individual, collective, profane, and sacred.

The socialization of the instinctive vision of the superconscious (too vulnerable to individual error) is a historical necessity that is based on the extraconscious functioning of the human psyche and on the immediate demands of the life of collectivities. Considered in the perspective of progressive adaptation, the religious institutions of the different nations correspond to an evolutionary stage of the species, which remains divided into social groups, each having to assure its own stabilization.

As the instinctive onirism of the superconscious loses its determining power—through multiplication of desires and under the assault of unleashed egotism—the communities, in order to continue to exist, inevitably have recourse to an institutional regulation, which, to be efficient, must necessarily be anchored in the original binding of each community that is the symbolic vision of values. But since this authentic vision withers, the unique means to consolidate it consists of creating a hypostasis of the values, which is, moreover, demanded by the belief in the real existence of deities. United in the belief, individuals are guided even in their intimate deliberation by values presented as a real transcendental imposition, with an absolute and eternal scope.

But the socialization of values—their hypostasis, which is inseparable from the hypostasis of deities and hope in real survival—inadequately produces the desired effect, which is the quieting of social anxiety and the conflict of deliberation. The cultural institution does not succeed in controlling the emergence of guilty anxiety. The participation in ceremonies of the cult, with its substitutive cleansing ritual, gives the communities' members the leisure to go about the profane occupations demanded by social life. Because the suggestive efficiency of ceremonies and their power to appease anxiety is not linked to its psychic cause (the creation of consoling determining factors) but to the intervention of deities, it reinforces the belief in their real existence. Insofar as the deities remain alive in people's beliefs, the life of communities is determined by the suggestive, somewhat obsessive force that results from the absolutism of values: Anxietude in all its forms and egocentricity remain sufficiently controlled—not to say repressed—which allows the communities to concentrate their effort on assuring their social organization.

This organization, under the protection of beliefs, becomes all the more an immediate necessity because the existence of each community is threatened by a constant environmental peril as the values and their ideal of harmonization are not authentically realized. Aggressiveness—more or less disciplined by the beliefs inside each cultural group—is unleashed toward the outer. Institutions, as they consolidate, confer upon the community material power and expansion. The multiplicity and the gravity of warring accidents eventually take from these historical events the accidental character that would suit them compared to the essential and the sacred, and confers upon them a character of pseudoessential importance.

But the consequences of the insufficient formulation of values are not exhausted by intersocial aggression. Within each society these consequences produce a similar effect of aggressive disorganization. The harshness of the battle for material goods eventually divides society members into oppressor and oppressed. The battle against social injustice imposes itself as a necessity. The defense of the primitive material security becomes an ideal of justice. But the affective overflow risks erasing the true cause of all these injustices, which is false justification, the disharmony with intimate determination, which rules everywhere and increases.

Under the assault of social injustices, the consoling belief of a justice after death gives way to doubt. The anxiety of doubt, seeking quieting, risks erring in the certainty that all higher values are inefficient. The result is the hypostasis of material values. Its consequence is the emergence of subconscious passions, from then on insufficiently repressed because of the error that wanted to eternalize higher values in declaring them absolute. Society falls apart following the destruction of its inadequate principle of union. The unique remedy seems to be an ideological reconstruction of the scale of values; but the effort of reconstruction, dictated by the aversion to the ancient spiritualist idealism, at best leads to idealist materialism. The hierarchy of values is reversed, the bottom is raised to the top. In relation to authentic spiritual values, the legitimate need for material security and the economical organization—as indispensable as they may be—are only a very desirable subfoundation for communities and their cultural life.

The more the higher values have been elevated as an absolute imposition, the more radical the absolutism of material values will be. The reversal of the spiritualist into the materialist utopia is the common characteristic of the period of downfall of all cultural epochs. This trait, however, is as much an indication of downfall (the exhaustion of animating vision) as a forerunner of renewal (the revision of the foundation). As utopias are defined by a search for satisfactions that are insufficiently founded upon real givens (forgetful as they are, either of the satisfaction of the basic material need or of authentic spiritual aspiration), renewal after the collapse of a culture has always been found by a return to authentic values: (Zoroaster, Lao-Tseu, Buddha, Jesus). The essential aspiration can be exhausted within individuals and even within a given community; it is inexhaustible in the collective life of the species. The spirit of truth imposes upon successive cultures, otherwise threatening to drown under anxiety-laden disarray, the effort to gradually better formulate the underlying psychological truth of all mythologies. Other peoples with a renewed mythical vision have relayed it from ancient peoples, the carriers of the flame, at the very moment their impulse collapsed. The impulse of surpassing is the unifying principle of all epochs and all cultures, so that the valid results acquired in the past are destined to fecundate the future.

From a biological point of view, the history of humanity as a whole is seen to be an uninterrupted effort to continue the evolutionary path that is characterized by the conflict between accidental anxietude and the various forms of essential anxiety. It is no less true that, when viewed in its accidental aspect, history seems to be merely the narrative of a dramatic chain of erroneous agitations and their resulting suffering. According to the shift of the emphasis of significance on one or the other of these aspects, the conditioning toward an excessive pessimism or an exalted idealism follows.

Can we possibly study anxiety and leave out of the field of investigation the most anxiety-laden phenomenon of life: death? The terrifying hold of death upon life is such that the collective attempts of repression and consolation—the beliefs and ideologies derived from myths—decide the cultural institutions and the cultural creations of all peoples composing humanity's past history. Confronting the problem of death and its anxiety therefore forces one to take a stance in relation to the guiding ideas that have repercussions in the current life of communities and forces one to be led into a domain where the most rooted prejudices and the most fanatical stands wage war.

Anxious about their pseudoscientific objectivity, human sciences have the tendency to stand aside from the essential problem. They carefully lock themselves into physiologism, sociologism, and pathologism. The pejorative term *psychologism*, on the other hand, has been invented to condemn the nonsubmission to the rule that imposes the abstinence of any critique of the ruling ideologies upon the psychologist.

But the resulting ideologies and activities are the product of psychic phenomena (thoughts, motives, desires, volitions). The entire life even in its most serious actuality depends upon the past evolution of psychic functions and the degree of lucidity they have attained. If current problems of life are without valid answers, it is because the psychic function of thought, with its affective blindness, does not succeed in elucidating them objectively. Is it not this objectivity that psychology should be anxious to attain, the objectivity that is acquired by the methodical study of the conditions of affective blinding and of elucidating thought, which would make it capable of confronting the problem of life efficiently? At this price only, the inner world science will assume its veracious role of becoming the science of life.

Since anxiety is the driving force of evolution, the genetic study of intrapsychic anxietude necessarily leads to the state of the evolutionary process that is, in fact, realized. To enter into the detailed analysis of actualities cannot belong to the aim of a general study of anxiety and its intimate causes. But nothing could be more natural than to encompass the opening perspectives in a general survey of the situation.

The link between anxiety of death and the inadequate solution of the collective problem has never been as evident as it is today. The entire world lives with the threat of annihilation while it is aware—more or less consciously—that mortal danger comes from a delay of the inner world science that remains incapable of controlling the misuse of the grandiose discoveries of physics. Indeed, even by overcoming the inhibiting anxiety—the anxiety of the intrapsyche—psychology could make up this delay only by the effort of generations as it is pursued—as physics has been—throughout centuries.

The only remaining hope is that the anxiety of the discoveries of physics eventually becomes greater than the anxiety of unveiling the psyche. The hope remains muffled and unattainable as long as it is countered by this generalized imposition that wants psychology never to be bold enough to study the secret of the psyche, for fear of finally unveiling each one's secret and everyone's repressed fault. Collective anxietude is certainly no exception to this general rule, according to which anxiety—unlike fear—does not refer directly to an external situation, but primarily to the disorientation provoked by the interruption of causal explanation. Only a systematic study of the intrapsyche can disclose the secret link between erring activity and subconscious motives. Beliefs and ideologies, as they seek solace for disorientation, eventually exacerbate collective anxiety, instead of elucidating its intimate causes.

Biologically speaking, the history of the entire species is at a decisive turn in what concerns the basic need for a satisfying preservation and the effort of elucidating adaptation. Sacred anxiety is exhausted and its impulse can no longer be reanimated by the emergence of a new mythical vision. Individuals and peoples have lost the capacity to feel imaginatively and to realize symbolically formulated values actively. Life is more than ever exposed to the multiple forms of accidental anxiety, a result of the multiplication of desires and artificial techniques of satisfaction (mechanization and propaganda). The individual and collective repression of guilty anxiety produces pathogenic explosions, and the resulting malaise of a worldwide magnitude is frequently called "collective psychosis." This situation evidently demands a reorganization of material life; but it demands even more imperatively the creation of essential support, the reformulation of guiding values. The greatness of the times—despite its dramatic decadence—resides in the fact that the need for elucidating adaptation forces it to elaborate, through all paths of research, the opening toward a veritable scientific era that would be free from superstition.

In the genetic point of view, past evolution authorizes the belief in future evolution. But it also demands that hope not be based on good intentions—which, most of the time, are wrong, pseudosublime motives—but only on the driving force of any evolution: the immanence of values or the transformational dynamism of anxiety.

NOTES

1. In Greek culture, for instance—as in all mythical cultures—deities illustrated psychic qualities: Zeus symbolized spirit; Hera, love; Athena, wisdom; Apollo, harmony; and so on. However, philosophy won't mention Zeus, Hera, Athena, Apollo at all; it will speak exclusively of the psychic qualities of spirit, love, wisdom, harmony, etc. So were the systems elaborated. Bearing the mark of all the splendor of Hellenic thought, these systems exerted a determining influence on the elite even though they remained speculative and contradictory be-

cause, while they endeavor to clarify psychic functioning, they were not based on any preliminary study of the lawful functioning of the psyche (for the study of which philosophical reflection prepared the way, but the instruments of which could be elaborated only throughout the centuries).

Because this philosophical explanation is only addressed only to the elite, it is preceded in all cultures by the theological explanation that is addressed to the crowds and that—in order to satisfy their primitive capacity of discernment—tends toward extreme simplification, the process of which is diametrically opposed to that of philosophical explanation. Theological exegesis no longer cares about the psychological problem that is the underlying truth of myths. Rather than speaking of spirit, love, wisdom, harmony, and the like theoretically, the theological systems represent the divinities who symbolize these qualities as really existing and truly immortal characters who really decide the fate of mortals.

References

Baruk, H. (1950). *Psychologie morale, experimentale, individuelle et sociale*. Paris: Presses Universitaires de France.

Boutonnier, J. (1945). *L'angoisse*. Paris: Presses Universitaires de France.

Descartes, R. (1949). *Discourse on Method*. Paris: Gallimard.

Diel, P. (1980). *Symbolism in Greek Mythology*. Boston: Shambhala.

Diel, P. (1986). *The God-Symbol: Its History and its Significance*. New York: Harper & Row.

Diel, P. (1989a). *The Psychology of Motivation*. Claremont, CA: Hunter House.

Diel, P. (1989b). *Psychology, Psychiatry, and Medicine*. Claremont, CA: Hunter House.

Dumas, G. (1946). Le supernaturel et les dieux d'apres les maladies mentales. In G. Dumas, *Essai de theorie pathologique*. Paris: Presses Universitaires de France.

Dumas, G. (1948). *La vie affective*. Paris: Presses Universitaires de France.

Freud, S. (1971). *Psychopathology of Everyday Life*. New York: W. W. Norton and Company, Inc.

Freud, S. (1950). *Ma vie et la psychanalyse* (M. Bonaparte, Trans.). Paris: Gallimard.

Hegel, G. (1966). *The Phenomenology of Mind* (J. B. Daille, Trans.). Atlantichighlands, N.J.: Humanities Press International.

Horney, K. (1942). *Self Analysis*. New York: Norton.

Janet, J. (1926). *De l'angoisse a l'extase*. Paris: Félix Alcan.

Jung, C. G. (1938). *Le moi et l'inconscient*. Paris: Gallimard.

Lange, J. (1895). *Essai sur les emotions* (G. Dumas, Trans.). Paris: Félix Alcan.

Pradines, M. (1946). *Traite de psychologie generale*. Paris: Presses Universitaires de France.

Ribot, T. (1925). *Psychologie des sentiments* (L. A. Terrier, Trans.). Paris: Félix Alcan.

Sully, J. (1904). *Le Rire*. Paris: Félix Alcan.

Other Books
by Paul Diel

BOOKS PUBLISHED BY EDITIONS PAYOT:

Le Symbolisme dans la Mythologie Grecque
(Symbolism in Greek Mythology) (Shambhala)

Le Divinité
(The God-Symbol) (Harper & Row)

Le Symbolisme dans le Bible
(Symbolism in the Bible) (Harper & Row)

Les Principes de l'Éducation et de la Rééducation
(The Psychology of Re-education) (Shambhala)

Le Symbolisme dans l'Evangile de Jean (by P. Diel and J. Solotareff)
(Symbolism in the Gospel of John) (Harper & Row)

BOOKS PUBLISHED BY OTHER PUBLISHERS IN FRANCE:

Journal d'une Psychanalyse
(*Journal of a Psychoanalysis*) (Shambhala)

Psychologie de la Motivation
(*The Psychology of Motivation*) (Hunter House Publishers)

Psychologie, Psychanalyse et Médecine
(*Psychology, Pychoanalysis and Medicine*)   (Hunter House Publishers)

ORDER FORM

10% DISCOUNT on orders of $20 or more —
20% DISCOUNT on orders of $50 or more —
30% DISCOUNT on orders of $250 or more —
On cost of books for fully prepaid orders

NAME

ADDRESS

CITY   STATE

ZIP   COUNTRY

TITLE	QTY	PRICE	TOTAL
Psychology of Motivation		@ $29.95	
Psychology, Psychoanalysis and Medicine		@ $24.95	
All Mighty		@ *	
Couples in Collusion		@ *	
Dynamics of Couples Therapy		@ *	
Intrance		@ *	
Trauma in the Lives of Children		@ *	
Other titles from the Hunter House catalog:			

* For current pricing, please call Hunter House
at (714) 624-2277

Shipping costs:
First book: $2.00
($3.00 for Canada)
Each additional
book: $.50 ($.75
for Canada)
For UPS rates and
bulk orders call us
at (714) 624-2277

TOTAL
Less discount @ _____%
TOTAL COST OF BOOKS
Calif. residents add sales tax
Shipping & handling
TOTAL ENCLOSED
Please pay in U.S. funds only

(   )

❑ Check   ❑ Money Order

Complete and mail to:

Hunter House Inc., Publishers

PO Box 847, Claremont, CA 91711

❑ Check here to receive our book catalog